The Pan Book of Wine and Beer Making

Ben Turner has been making wine since 1945 and brewing beer since 1952. He has played a leading role in the growth of this movement and is a Past President of both the National Association of Wine & Beermakers and the National Guild of Wine & Beer Judges. He has been writing, lecturing and broadcasting on home-brew topics since 1958.

The Pan Book of Wine and Beer Making

BEN TURNER

colour photographs by Trevor Haywood

Pan Books
London and Sydney

First published 1964 as *Improve Your Winemaking* by Pelham Books Ltd
Published 1965 as *The Pan Book of Winemaking* by Pan Books Ltd
reprinted five times
Revised 1976
reprinted three times
This completely revised edition published 1984 by Pan Books Ltd,
Cavaye Place, London SW10 9PG
9 8 7 6 5 4 3 2

ISBN 0 330 28245 X

Photoset by Parker Typesetting Service, Leicester
Printed and bound in Great Britain by
Cox & Wyman Ltd, Reading

Contents

Introduction

Wine-, mead-, beer- and cider-making all began in the home. There is a belief that wine-making was the first of these four to be organized on a commercial basis in the Middle East. Trading in wine made from grapes has a very long history; but date wine was known to the early Egyptians, and the Greeks were masters at mixing honey, fruit juices, herbs and pine cones with their grape juices to make different wines.

Cider, too, has a long and noble history. It was well known in Biblical days when the sandy deserts of the present Middle East were flourishing green fields and trees.

In Britain ale houses have been in existence since the Romans arrived in 54 BC, and mead was made by every household which kept bees – an enormous number since bees provided both honey for sweetening and wax for candles. The quality of these beverages may be questionable but the indisputable fact remains that drunkenness was rife.

Country wine-making, as opposed to the making of mead and melomels, really got going in Britain when the West Indies were colonized and cheap sugar was imported by the shipload. There were then, as now, two schools of thought. One group made wines from the fruits, vegetables and flowers of the countryside, while the other made imitation clarets, burgundies, hocks and the like. This is evidenced by the many recipes published in the eighteenth and nineteenth centuries. Yet the Industrial Revolution caused a great movement of people from the countryside to the towns and slowly the home-brew crafts virtually died out. Only after the Second World War did home-brewing begin to revive, in spite of the many shortages of the period, particularly that of sugar (rationed until 1952).

Since then the movement has grown dramatically and reliable estimates suggest that around four million people in the United Kingdom make wine, beer, mead or cider every year. Many of them regularly make their beverages from kits, but as many as two million or more make their wines from fruits, vegetables and flowers that they have grown or gathered. Although the wines and beers made from kits are good and enjoyable, they provide nothing like the satisfaction of those made from fresh ingredients.

With so many people making their own wine and beer, a new industry has been developed to provide specialist equipment that helps to make home-brew activities more successful and easier; the various chemical ingredients from sterilizing agents upwards are being packaged in appropriate quantities and marketed for use in the home.

It has even developed into a social activity, with the growth of wine-making clubs, in most villages and towns, not only in the UK but more recently in Australia, Belgium, Canada, Holland, South Africa and the USA. As a hobby, wine-making and brewing at home frequently introduces the participant to new and lasting friendships.

The quality of wines and beers that can be produced at home is closely related to the trouble taken. The use of good equipment and ingredients supported by sound knowledge is likely to produce the best wines and beers. As with everything else in life – the more you put into the making of your wines and beers, the more you will get out of them in quality, enjoyment and satisfaction.

Author's note

You are urged to read the chapters prior to the recipes to ensure an understanding of the equipment needed, the ingredients used and the activities involved. With cleanliness and care you can produce enjoyable beverages from the start.

Making your own wines and beers can enrich your life-style. A glass of your own wine with a meal brings graciousness into living. A glass of beer that you have brewed yourself provides a satisfaction that you will surely enjoy. At a few pence per bottle both are well within your means.

Glossary for wine-making

acetic The smell and taste of acetic acid – vinegar – sometimes found in wines that have been contaminated.
acid In wine, mead, and cider the inclusion of sufficient acid is essential for bouquet and flavour. The three main acids used are citric, malic and tartaric but other acids are formed during fermentation.
activated yeast Dried yeast granules that have been rehydrated and made viable.
airlock A simple device for excluding air from a fermenting must whilst permitting the fermentation gas to escape.
alcohol The spirit, mostly ethanol, produced from sugar by yeast during fermentation.
aroma The odour given off by the main ingredient in a wine, whether fruit, flower or vegetable.
bentonite A grey powder widely used for fining wines.
bouquet The complex collection of odours given off by a finished wine, mead or cider. It consists of different esters, alcohols and acids.
Campden tablet Sodium metabisulphite powder compressed into a small tablet. Widely used for sterilizing equipment and for inhibiting oxidation and the development of micro-organisms.
carbon dioxide The name of the gas given off during fermentation. Sometimes referred to as CO_2.
demijohn A colourless glass jar with a narrow neck supported by two glass carrying rings. The jar is of a nominal 1 gallon/4.5 litres capacity but frequently varies up to 8½ pints/4.8 litres.
dry A wine, mead or cider without trace of sweetness.
enzymes Substances secreted by yeast that cause sugar to change into alcohol and carbon dioxide.

ester A fragrant odour created by the interaction of organic acids and alcohols.

ferment The action of converting sugar into alcohol and carbon dioxide.

fermentation-on-the-pulp The action of converting sugar to alcohol and carbon dioxide in the presence of crushed fruit. This action also assists in the extraction of colour, flavour, acids and other substances.

ferment-on The addition of sugar or syrup to a must to continue the fermentation and so increase the quantity of alcohol produced.

ferment-out Leaving a must to continue fermenting until all the sugar has been converted to alcohol and carbon dioxide.

fining The precipitation of solid particles in suspension by the addition of a neutral agent such as bentonite. It clarifies the previously hazy beverage.

fungal amylase One of the diastase enzymes that convert starch into sugar. Used to clarify a wine that contains a starch haze or one made from cereals.

hydrometer An instrument for measuring the quantity of sugar in a must and for this reason sometimes called a saccharometer.

invert sugar A simple *mixture* of the two single sugars, fructose and glucose, as opposed to sucrose (household sugar) which is a *combination* of the two sugars. Sucrose is not immediately fermentable but wine yeast contains an enzyme called invertase which separates the two sugars so that they can then be fermented separately. Invert sugar can be made in the home by boiling household sugar in water containing a little citric acid for 20 minutes.

lead glaze Earthenware jars and pots used to be glazed with molten lead to make them waterproof. However, we now know that the acid in fruits and wines reacts with the lead to form a poisonous salt that can cause death. Very old vessels of this kind should not be used. They can be recognized by a softness when pressed with a sharp object and by a dull sound when struck. Modern earthenware jars are glazed with an inert substance that is perfectly safe. The glaze is hard and the vessel rings when struck.

lees Another name for sediment. The solid matter that sinks to the bottom of a vessel when a fermented beverage clears.

lugs The name given to the two glass rings that support the neck of a demijohn.

malo-lactic ferment The conversion of malic acid to lactic acid by bacteria. It usually occurs in red fruit wines after fermentation is finished, sometimes after bottling. The wine tastes softer and less sharp, but some carbon dioxide is also produced which can cause unwanted effervescence, or even blow a cork. It can be prevented by the addition of sulphite at the rate of 50 parts per million, i.e. one Campden tablet per gallon of wine.

must The name given to a solution, whether containing pulp or not, that is in process of being converted into wine, mead or cider.

nutrient Mineral salts containing nitrogen required by yeast in the process of fermentation.

oxidized A beverage to which so much oxygen has been admitted that it loses vitality and develops a dull, flat taste. The beverage is in fact over-oxidized.

pectin A substance found in most fruits, usually in the membrane containing the minute drops of juice. It can cause a haze in the finished wine.
pectic enzyme An enzyme added to crushed fruit in the form of a white powder or a brown liquid to break down the pectin, release the juice and prevent haze. Instructions for its use are given on the package.
proof spirit The alcohol content of a beverage is sometimes expressed in degrees proof. It can be converted into percentage of volume by dividing by 7 and multiplying by 4. Thus a vodka of 70° proof contains 40 per cent alcohol. Polish spirit is usually twice as strong and is usually sold at 140° proof, i.e. 80 per cent alcohol.
punt The indentation on the bottom of a wine bottle. At one time they used to be quite deep but on modern bottles they are fairly shallow. Bottle sediment frequently collects in them, so make sure that the punt of a previously used bottle is well cleaned before it is used again.
racking see **siphon**.
saccharin A non-fermentable sweetening agent. Avoid it in fruit juices and canned fruits from which you wish to make a dry wine. Conversely add it to a dry wine to sweeten it slightly. One, or at most two, saccharin pellets crushed and added to a bottle just prior to serving is usually enough. Sweetex, Hermesetas or other brands of saccharin pellets may be used.
sediment Particles of pulp, dead yeast cells and other organic and inorganic debris deposited on the bottom of a vessel in which a beverage has been fermented or matured.
siphon The instrument used to remove a clear or clearing wine from a deposit of sediment. The same word is also used to describe the action itself, which is also called racking.
specific gravity The density or weight of a substance compared with the weight of the same volume of water at a prescribed temperature. The hydrometer measures the specific gravity of a must or wine from which can be calculated the weight of the sugar therein. Wine-makers usually refer to specific gravity than to grams or ounces of sugar.
spoilage organisms Micro-organisms invisible to the naked eye that float in the air and cause an unpleasant odour and taint in a must or wine unless prevented from doing so. They include bacteria, fungi and moulds.
sulphite The short name for metabisulphite used for sterilizing equipment and protecting musts and wines. In solution it releases sulphur dioxide, long known as a bactericide.
thin A beverage with little substance to it, watery.
vinosity The wine-like bouquet and taste in a beverage.

Equipment

For those who have never made wine before, a number of companies market a 'beginner's kit'. The actual contents may vary slightly but the following items are usually included: a colourless glass demijohn with a nominal capacity of one gallon, although sometimes this amounts to 4.8 litres/8½ pints; a polythene funnel; a bored bung and an airlock; a length of plastic tubing to use as a siphon; six wine bottles and corks; a container of concentrated grape juice compound; a sachet of dried yeast granules; crystals to make a sterilizing solution and some Campden tablets.

The equipment can be used time and time again. It is the minimum to get you started and you will soon want to add some other very useful pieces so that you can make wines from fresh fruits, flowers, vegetables and so on.

All the equipment mentioned in this book can be obtained from most of the 1,000 or so home brew specialist shops to be found in nearly every town. The larger branches of Boots and some of their smaller branches stock a wide range of equipment, or can order it for you from their central warehouse if you ask them. Some pieces of equipment are also available from branches of Woolworth's, large supermarkets, do-it-yourself centres and even garden centres. If you live far away from any of these sources of supply you could write to one of the several mail-order houses advertising in the magnificent monthly magazine *Amateur Winemaker & Brewer*, published by Mr C. J. J. Berry, from South Street, Andover, Hampshire.

A natural *polythene bin* is the first item that you should acquire. Buy one with a lid, a carrying handle, and with graduated quantity markings on the side. Bins are available in several sizes, but 10, 15 and 25 litres are the most popular. You need at least one bin and it should always be larger than the quantity of wine you are making so that there is no spillage when you move it. These bins are not only light to handle and easy to clean, but also inert to acids and alkalis and therefore safe to use for making wine. You will need one for mixing musts; as a container in which to crush fruit; as a fermenting vessel for the extraction of colour, acids, sugars, tannins, minerals and vitamins from fruits; as a receptacle when racking a wine that has to be returned to its original jar for maturation; even for the storage of small pieces of equipment when not in use. A long-handled *plastic spoon* or paddle will be needed to stir the must.

A *strainer* that fits across the bin, with interchangeable coarse or fine meshes, is available, as well as nylon *straining bags*, coarse or fine mesh, and in small and large sizes. One or the other is essential for straining out solid particles.

A *brown glass demijohn* is useful for storing wines. The brown glass keeps out the light and prevents the colour of the wine from fading. *Cork* or *rubber bungs* should be used to seal these jars, but a bung with a safety device should be used if there is the least risk of any re-fermentation.

Demijohn labels that clip on to the lugs of the jars are useful for keeping note of the contents of the jars, both during fermentation and storage. They are re-usable.

Bottles and jars can be cleaned more effectively with a *long-handled brush*. They are especially effective for cleaning the punt of a bottle and under the shoulder of a demijohn. During fermentation dead yeast cells and fruit pulp often form a ring in this position that is otherwise difficult to dislodge.

When more than 4½ litres/1 gallon of wine is to be made at a time, a larger *polythene fermenter* can be bought that holds up to 25 litres. Glass jars in protective wicker or plastic baskets are equally useful. They all have openings suitable for taking a *bored bung* and *airlock*. The bungs are available in rubber as well as the traditional cork. Airlocks are marketed in a variety of shapes made from glass or plastic. The bored bung should always be screwed on to the stem of the airlock, after it has been soaked in warm water to soften it. Never attempt to push a dry bung on to the stem of a glass lock; the probability is that the glass will break and cut your hand. Always use a soft wet bung and a screwing action for safety. Even so, hold glass locks in a cloth – just in case.

Several sizes of polythene *funnel* may be required from time to time: small ones that fit into the neck of a bottle; larger ones for jars. Try to obtain funnels with a ridge down the outside of the outlet tube. This allows the air in the bottle or jar to escape while it is being filled. Without a ridge of some sort the funnel often seals the container so effectively that the liquid poured into it cannot pass through.

Siphons can be more sophisticated than just a length of tubing. Glass tubes in the shape of the letter 'J' can be attached to the end that goes into the vessel to be emptied. The shape of the tube causes the wine to be sucked down from above rather than up from the sediment. With such an instrument more of the clear wine can be removed from the sediment without disturbance. An alternative version consists of a plastic tube that has a 1 cm/½ in block at one end. Just above the blockage, four holes are bored about 2.5 mm/$^1/_{10}$ in in diameter. The open end of the tube is pushed into one end of the siphon tube proper. The result of this is to cause the wine to flow across the sediment into the tube, again without disturbing it.

In both cases the bottom of the J-tube or the bottom of the blocked end can be rested on the bottom of the demijohn. It can be held there firmly, and without fear of it moving, by first threading a bored bung containing a vent hole on to the tube. This bung can be pushed into the neck of the jar while the entry end of the tube is still high in the wine. When the bung is tight, the tube can be gently pushed down until it touches the bottom of the jar. The important factor to remember is the vent hole. Without this, suction is not possible, for it is essential that air takes the place of the wine as it is removed.

At the other end of the tube a *small tap* can be fitted so that the speed of the outflow is controlled. When filling bottles, the flow can be temporarily stopped when one bottle is full and the siphon is moved to the next bottle.

It is difficult to squeeze the plastic tube sufficiently tightly to prevent spillage. If a tap is not fitted, a short length of rubber tubing could be pushed on to the plastic; the rubber is more pliable and easier to seal by squeezing between finger and thumb. Some siphons come complete with suitable entry and exit facilities and even with a pump in the middle for filling the tube without your having to suck at the exit end.

A long kitchen *thermometer* with graduations from 0–100°C/32–212°F is most useful for checking the temperature of tepid water before reactivating dried yeast granules; of must before adding the yeast; of must and wine before checking its specific gravity; or of must that is cooling prior to the addition of pectic enzyme and sulphite.

Similarly, there are great advantages in using a *hydrometer* and *trial jar* to check specific gravity of musts and newly-finished wines. The hydrometer looks rather like a thermometer. Its graduation marks range from 0.990 to 1.150, and when floated in a liquid the hydrometer indicates the gravity or weight of that liquid compared with the same volume of water at 15°C/59°F. The additional weight is mainly sugar, although some acids, minerals and other elements may be present in small to minute quantities. Detailed information on the use of the hydrometer is given in the chapter beginning on page 57. Sufficient here to indicate its importance in measuring the quantity of sugar present in a must or wine.

As far as possible, the temperature of a fermenting must should be kept steady. Many houses now have adequate warmth day and night from central heating systems, but not all. If you have no such facility you may find it helpful to use a *heating tray* sufficient for two demijohns to stand upon. Alternatively, you might prefer to encircle your jar with a *heating belt*. Yet another way is to insert an *immersion heater* in your jar of must. All of these instruments are usually fitted with a thermostat to prevent over-heating.

Most wines clear by themselves, or with the assistance of some finings, but occasionally a wine with an extra special polish is required, perhaps for an exhibition or competition. A number of *filter kits* are now available for this purpose. Some come with pads like blotting paper; others use a combination of chemicals and a calico bag that fit into a bin that sits on top of a receiving jar. Other filters have a connection that can be fitted to a tap to create a vacuum and cause faster filtering. Whatever system you use follow the instructions carefully to avoid over exposure of the wine to the air.

Only proper *wine bottles* should be used. Coloured glass protects the wine from fading and is especially useful for red wines. Any bottles that have been used before should be thoroughly washed and sterilized before re-use. Remove old labels by soaking them off rather than by scratching them off. Attractive new *labels and collars* can be stuck on when the bottles are full. *Cylindrical corks* are best for wines that are to be stored on their sides. The longer you intend to mature the wine in bottles, the better the corks should be. Never use cylindrical corks a second time, especially if they have been pierced with a corkscrew. Always soften them for some hours in a sulphite solution and ram them home with a *corking tool*. There is a wide selection of tools from which to choose.

A coloured *foil* or *plastic capsule* can be pressed over the top of the cork and the neck of the bottle to present a professional finish to the wine.

Ideally, the bottles should be stored in a *wine rack* in a cool dark place. Each wine-maker must find the most suitable place in their own home.

Last but by no means least, for it should be started at the very outset, is a *wine record book*. The most popular kind is a loose-leaf folder containing a number of cards in which it is only necessary to fill in the relevant data. This includes the details of ingredients, sugar, acid, etc., date started, specific gravity, dates finished, racked, stored, and so on.

The largest and most expensive piece of equipment is a *fruit press*. This is of immense help when wine is being made from larger fruits, such as apples and pears. It is also of great help when making large quantities of wine from soft fruit such as blackberries, elderberries, gooseberries, grapes, peaches, rhubarb and so on. A mechanical *crusher* can also be bought, but leave that until you are making a hundred gallons or more at a time!

A *cask* is of great value for maturing red wines. The minimum size which it is safe to use is 25 litres/5½ gallons. Before use a cask should be thoroughly soaked in a sulphite solution while the staves swell and become liquid-tight. Use only new or reconditioned casks that have previously held wine or spirit. Never use an old cask that has lain empty and neglected, nor one that has ever contained vinegar, beer, or any chemical. Stand the cask in a cradle so that the tap can be used easily and the belly staves are not in contact with a surface.

Clear glass *decanters* are more attractive than bottles on the dining table and allow the wine a chance to breathe before being poured into glasses. Many wines throw a deposit during bottle storage and the clear wine should be removed to a decanter before the wine is served.

Tulip-shaped *glasses* are most suitable for white wines, and spherical goblets for red wines. All glasses should be plain and uncoloured to show off the wine to its best advantage.

Hygiene

In the past, home-made wines and beers often contained an unpleasant smell or taste that, in the wines, was frequently masked by adding sugar and brandy. We now know that the main cause of these off-flavours was inadequate attention to hygiene by the use of unsterilized ingredients and containers. Former sauce and squash bottles were often used, or else wine bottles that contained the dregs of previous contents. Even corks were pressed into repeated use until they disintegrated. Wooden spoons used for jams and pickles were also used to stir wine musts or beer worts. Sieves, funnels and containers in general use were all 'borrowed' for making wine and beer. Over-ripe or mouldy ingredients not thought to be suitable for other uses were allocated to the wine. Buying long-harvested fruit left exposed on market stalls and sold cheaply on a Saturday night was regarded as the way to make wine at home.

During the making, containers were often left uncovered, or at best, draped with a thin muslin cloth that kept out only the largest of flies and none of the spoilage organisms that could not be seen, but which we now know were always present, floating in the air and carried on the feet of tiny fruit flies. Fruit was often left soaking in water for up to three weeks until a mouldy growth had appeared on the surface. Far too much sugar was then used and when the fermentation, often in a large water-jug, was finished, it would be left on its sediment until it cleared. Meanwhile, the wine absorbed the putrefying flavours of decomposing yeast cells and particles of pulp.

There were many recipes available, sometimes in books that never mentioned hygiene as we now understand the word. The practice of good hygiene in wine-making and brewing and in cider- and mead-making, too, prevents most problems and enhances the bouquet and flavour of the beverage. It not only enables all the natural flavours to come through unspoiled, but allows the yeast to ferment without interference from other fungi and bacteria.

Essentially, all equipment used for making wine and beer should be kept exclusively for those purposes and should not be in general use. For example, a plastic bucket used in the making of wine or beer should never be used for soaking dirty clothes, let alone washing the car! Furthermore, it is strongly recommended that you only purchase equipment that has been made specifically for making wine or beer. Purpose-made equipment is constructed from safe materials including glass, stainless steel and natural polythene. Coloured polythene may contain some injurious element such as cadmium.

Second-hand equipment is always something of a risk, especially second-hand casks, which are best avoided unless they have been properly reconditioned. Bungs and stoppers should be made from plastic, rubber or good quality cork, but always give those made from cork an overnight soak in a sulphite solution before use so that it can soak right into the pores.

Containers used for pulp fermentation and for mixing ingredients should be made from natural polythene. This is inert to acids and alkalis, light to handle and easy to clean. These containers usually come with a good fitting lid. Avoid all metal containers other than stainless steel. Copper, iron and brass react with the acids in wine and create injurious compounds. Wood, in the form of oak, is safe and even beneficial, but it is heavy to handle and difficult to clean and sterilize. Glazed earthenware may be used but do make sure that the glazing agent wasn't lead, for that will react with the acids and create poisons.

Always leave sufficient headspace in these containers so that the contents are not spilled when being moved. The polythene bins have proper carrying handles for this purpose. If a lid is provided keep it on the container at all times other than when you are filling, stirring or emptying it. Even then, do your best to see that the contents are not exposed for longer than is necessary.

When musts or worts, wines or beers are left in contact with a surface such as a bin, jar or bottle for some time, tiny pieces of pigment become imbedded. Deposits of tartrate, proteins and other organic debris settle firmly in awkward places. They should all be scrubbed off with a long-handled brush that will reach into the punt of a wine bottle, as well as under the shoulder. Similarly with demijohns, the undersurface of the shoulder needs a special clean. Green and brown bottles and jars should be held up to a strong light and examined to make sure that all sediment has been removed. After a piece of equipment has been in use for a year or longer, it may need a special clean. Bottles and jars can be filled with a weak solution of Chempro or bleach and left overnight, or until their original freshness has returned. Rinse these thoroughly with plenty of cold water. This treatment is especially necessary for decanters that are in frequent use. It is much more satisfactory than any of the former methods for cleaning them. New equipment should also be washed and sterilized before use, no matter how well it has been packed. It may well have been in contact with invisible spoilage organisms before being packed. Cleaning can be performed with hot water and detergent, well rinsed off with plenty of cold water.

A satisfactory sterilizing solution for equipment can be made by dissolving one level teaspoonful of sodium metabisulphite and an equal quantity of citric acid in 500 ml/a scant pint of cold water. Sulphur dioxide is produced which, together with the acid, acts as a powerful bactericide. Some fumes are given off that are rather pungent and care should be taken not to breathe them in while pouring the sterilizing solution from one container to another or while swirling it round a bin. Provided all the equipment is already clean, the solution may be used throughout a single session of activity, but it will not keep from one day to another. Every surface likely to come into contact with the wine, beer, mead or cider should be sterilized. Surfaces, no matter from what they are made, are never perfectly smooth. Under the microscope minute caverns can be seen that are large enough to hold spoilage organisms. The surfaces must, therefore, have the solution passed over them several times to ensure that each invisible hole is filled. The solution may be poured from a bin to a demijohn, then to a hydrometer and trial jar through a funnel. The siphon should be filled and the exterior of the two ends also treated; the plastic stirrer, the thermometer, straining bag, sieve, bottle brush, bottles, stoppers, corks, bungs and airlocks should all be sterilized before use; nothing should be missed. Drain any surplus solution back into the jug or bottle in which it was made and this should be used at the end for wiping down work surfaces and the floor where spillages may have occurred.

After sterilizing a piece of equipment, it should be used as soon as possible and whilst still damp, for the trace of sulphur dioxide will not harm the must or wort, or finished wine or beer.

When not in use containers should be stored in a clean and dry place. Straining bags should be kept in a polythene bag, small equipment in suitable boxes; jars should be kept plugged with cotton wool, if only to keep out flies, wasps, spiders or even mice! Lids should be fitted on to bins and in general all equipment should be cared for and kept orderly and neat.

Attention to these matters is far less onerous in practice than it may seem and saves so much time and trouble.

Equal care should be taken with all ingredients used. Yeasts should always be kept in sealed sachets stored in the refrigerator; acids, nutrients, enzymes, tannin, sulphite, etc. should be kept in securely sealed screw-stoppered jars. Keep them in a drawer or cupboard away from other household goods. Buy only a sufficient quantity of any item for a single season. None of these items keep indefinitely, especially in half-filled containers. It is better to buy fresh stock every year.

Major ingredients should be used as soon as obtained, or else prepared and frozen until required. Never leave ingredients lying around exposed to the air. Flowers and leaves quickly wilt and are past their best within a few hours. Soft fruits have a very short life, too, and quickly form mouldy clumps. The larger fruits like apples and pears, will keep for some weeks if spread out on a tray in a dry, cool, dark and airy place. Avoid all damp and humid storage for this is beloved by moulds that are always present in the air.

Remove and discard all stalks and bruised or damaged portions of fruit, then wash the sound fruit in a weak sulphite solution. This can be prepared by dissolving two crushed Campden tablets in 4.5 litres/1 gallon of water, or one tablet in 2.25 litres/½ gallon for a lesser quantity. Although Campden tablets are not expensive, the sulphite from which they are made is even cheaper. You can dissolve 25 g of sulphite in 250 ml of cold boiled water (1 oz in half a pint), and store this in a screw-stoppered bottle in a cool dark place. One 5 ml teaspoonful of this solution is the equivalent of one Campden tablet. This volume of solution is equal to 50 Campden tablets and will keep for three or four months.

After washing the fruit, crush it and remove any stones, add water as required and one Campden tablet, or its equivalent, per 4.5 litres/1 gallon of wine being made. This effectively inhibits the growth of all moulds, fungi and bacteria including wine yeast. The must is thus as clean and as sterilized as the container. It is clearly imperative to keep the container with the must in it closely covered so that it remains uncontaminated. To examine under the microscope a droplet of must left exposed to the air is like seeing shoals of different fish swimming in the sea.

During fermentation the carbon dioxide, being slightly heavier than air, lies on the surface of the must if it is not disturbed. As the quantity of gas builds up it has to escape into the atmosphere. Although tight fitting, few polythene lids are gas-proof. Even so, some provision should be made so that the gas can escape. When the must is poured into a demijohn an airlock filled with a sulphite solution should be fitted.

As soon as it is evident that fermentation is quite finished the beverage should be removed from its sediment. The dead or dying yeast cells and the insoluble particles of organic material will gradually decompose and impart a most unpleasant odour and flavour otherwise.

Storage jars should be topped up and kept full and well-sealed to exclude air-borne spoilage organisms. Failure to do this may well result in a thin skin of a white powdery substance forming on the surface of the wine, mead, beer or cider, more especially if the beverage is also low in acid and alcohol. Air must be excluded at all times to avoid off flavours.

In modern wineries the grape juice never comes into contact with the air from the moment the grape is crushed until the moment the mature wine is poured into a glass to be drunk. Similarly with modern breweries. It makes sound sense and prevents spoilage.

Wine from kits

Concentrated grape juice has been used since the beginning of the century to make British wine commercially. It produces a fairly strong wine that is so sweetened and flavoured that it appeals to a great many people not accustomed to drinking imported French or German table wines. In the late 1950s Spanish concentrated grape juice was marketed in cans small enough to be of use to the home wine-maker. Soon other companies saw the potential and the wine kit as we know it today was created. There is now a very wide range of different wine types available in kit form as well as four distinct quality bands. A good number of other fruit juices have also been concentrated and marketed in kit form. The choice is now very wide indeed, as an inspection of the shelves of a good 'home-brew' centre will show.

Essentially a wine kit consists of concentrated grape and/or other fruit juice, adjusted as may be necessary with acid and flavouring. Most of them are marketed in 1 kg/2¼ lb cans, but a number are sold in 560 ml/1 pint plastic bottles. The concentrate has only to be diluted with water, further sweetened with sugar and fermented with yeast to produce six standard size bottles of wine. Each container bears a label giving step by step instructions on how to make up the wine. The minimum of equipment is required, the method is very easy and involves little effort. Indeed, the author has helped blind people to make and enjoy wine from kits.

Before buying a kit, it is worth knowing about the different qualities. They are as follows:

Superior These kits consist of concentrated grape juice made from wine grapes grown in good wine-producing areas of Spain, France and Italy. The juice is very carefully concentrated to ensure the minimum caramelization of the grape sugars. No additional sugar is required and no artificial flavouring is added. These are the most expensive kits to buy but they produce a wine that is not far below the commercial counterpart and costs about one fifth of the price. The CWE Connoisseur range is the best known example of this quality, but Boots and a number of other manufacturers market similar kits.

Standard These kits are sometimes described as grape juice compounds because they may include certain sugars and flavourings. Additional sugar is always required during fermentation. Less expensive than the 'Superior' range they nevertheless produce a very satisfactory wine in a great number of different styles. Because of EEC regulations, the traditional names of Sauternes, Hock, Port, Sherry, Burgundy, Claret, etc. may not be used by the manufacturers to describe the styles of wines available, but the results are not too dissimilar if the instructions are carefully followed.

Budget These compounds have been devised to sell at a very economical price. They may contain a mixture of fruit juices as well as sugars and flavourings. Additional sugar will be required during fermentation. The result is still an enjoyable, everyday quality beverage that can be good value for money.

Express These compounds often contain little, if any, grape juice although apple juice is often included. Sugars and flavourings are present and additional sugar is required during fermentation. Other chemicals are provided to stimulate fermentation and, subsequently, to stabilize the wine so that it can be consumed within three or four weeks of starting it off. The result is a wine that makes pleasant quaffing. For this reason it is sometimes available in kits that produce thirty bottles rather than six.

'Country wine kits' are also available. They produce the traditional blackberry, elderberry, bilberry, apple, orange and other wines that people who have no access to grapes like to make.

Some kits come with a sachet of dried yeast granules, and some manufacturers even include six attractive bottle labels. Although not essential, experience shows that the yeast provided often benefits from the addition of a level teaspoonful of nutrient. This stimulates fermentation and ensures the maximum production of alcohol.

Instructions on how to make up the kits vary slightly from one manufacturer to another and, in the first instance at least, these should be carefully followed. In general, the instructions are much as follows:

1 Make up a sterilizing solution of sodium metabisulphite and citric acid (see the chapter on hygiene, page 19), and carefully sterilize a glass demijohn, bored bung, airlock and a funnel.
2 Drain out the demijohn, place the funnel in the neck of the jar and pour in four or five pints of cold water. If your tap water is known to contain chlorine, it is better to boil it in an open pan and allow it to cool before use.
3 Open the container of concentrate and empty this into the jar. Rinse out the container with a little more water to ensure that no concentrate is wasted. Leave a gap under the mouth of the jar for about a further 560 ml/1 pint of water.

The instructions now usually require the addition of yeast granules (sometimes provided) to the jar. The must will begin to ferment more quickly, however, if the dried yeast is first activated in half a cupful of tepid water (between 40–45°C/104–113°F), for about fifteen minutes and then added to the jar with the yeast nutrient.
4 The airlock, fitted into a softened bored bung, is then filled with a sulphite solution or plain boiled water and screwed into the neck of the jar.
5 Leave the jar in a warm place, 21–5°C/70–77°F, for a day or two until the tumultuous ferment is finished. Much froth may be made and if the jar is too full it will boil over, making a mess around the jar. The instructions usually recommend leaving the jar in a warm place. This is effective for red wines, but the flavour of white wines is often enhanced by continuing the fermentation in a somewhat cooler atmosphere, say 16–18°C/61–5°F.
6 After seven to ten days, take out the airlock, pour some must into a sterilized jug or basin, stir in the required amount of sugar, and return the must to the jar.

A better way is to dissolve the sugar in a little hot water and, when it is cool, to pour this into the jar. More water should now be added to raise the level of must in the jar to within 3 cm/1¼ in of the bottom of the bung which should then be replaced.
7 After a few weeks, the tiny bubbles rising in the must will cease and the young wine will begin to clear from the neck downwards, depositing a sediment of dead yeast cells and fruit pulp on the bottom

of the jar. As soon as it can be seen that fermentation has finished, the instructions usually recommend you to add one or two crushed Campden tablets to the wine, and to siphon it into a sterilized storage jar for a few weeks, until the wine has cleared to brightness. It is often more effective, however, to add the Campden tablet(s) and to move the jar to the coldest place you can find for about a week, preferably to stand on a concrete or stone-tiled floor. This reduces the thermal movements in the jar and encourages the suspended particles to settle more quickly and firmly on the bottom of the jar.

If the wine is now clear, it can be siphoned straight into sterilized bottles, corked, labelled and stored for a few months to mature. The wine will continue to improve for at least six months and will keep for several years. If it is still hazy, it should be racked into another jar, topped up and left in a cold place until the wine is bright.

A great many people are well satisfied with the wine they make from kits. If you have never made wine before you are strongly recommended to make up several of these kits to gain a little experience. The wines produced from the kits naturally vary slightly. Each manufacturer formulates his kits to produce wines that in his opinion are similar in style to a comparable commercial wine. But palates vary and you should compare the products of different manufacturers and decide for yourself the one you prefer.

Whilst enjoyable wines can be made from kits, they do not present much of a challenge. After a while, you may well want to make some wine from the fruits of the countryside. The taste of these wines may differ from that of the kits, but the quality can be every bit as good. Indeed, with some experience you may find that you can make even better wines. The satisfaction of having made them yourself from the fruit to the glass will be even greater.

Essential ingredients

Apart from the main flavour-making ingredient, such as elderberries, a number of other items are essential to the making of a sound, balanced wine. These include water, acid, tannin, sugar, yeast and yeast nutrient.

The sources that supply equipment that are detailed on page 12 also supply the acids, tannins, yeasts and nutrients. All your other needs for sterilizing agents, pectin reducing enzymes, wine stabilizers, acid testing, fining and even non-fermentable sweetening agents can also be supplied from the home brew centres and similar sources.

Water Most tap water is suitable for wine-making, although if it is chlorinated at source then it is best to boil it vigorously in an open pan for a minute or two so that the chlorine is driven off. Hard water with its higher mineral content probably has some advantage over soft water, but the most suitable base ingredients usually contain a sufficient mixture of minerals. The position can be further improved by the inclusion of some grape.

Spring water is usually excellent, and well water is normally suitable also. The well should be positioned far away from possible contamination by drainage into it of waste matter that may be injurious. Rain water may be used after it has been passed through a filter and then boiled for five minutes. It is extremely soft and needs the addition of minerals and trace elements from fruits. Distilled water is not normally suitable because it is so pure and free from these important elements. Bottled spa water used for everyday drinking is expensive but may be used if you so wish.

Acid The three main organic acids found in fruits are citric, malic and tartaric. Citric is the cheapest and most widely used. It imparts a rather sharp taste but can be used in the form of freshly expressed lemon juice or white crystals. Malic acid imparts a pleasant, fruity taste, but after fermentation is finished, and even when the wine has been bottled for a while, some of the malic acid is subject to conversion into lactic acid by bacteria. Carbon dioxide is given off and can be the cause of a blown cork or even a burst bottle. Tartaric acid is popular with the *cognoscenti* of amateur wine-makers because it is the main acid found in grapes. During maturation of the wine, especially if it is stored in a very cold place – even for a short while – some of the tartaric acid combines with potassium in the wine and is precipitated in the form of tiny glass-like crystals of potassium tartrate. These often cling to the end of the cork, or side of the bottle, or deep in the punt. The wine is disfigured marginally but is none the worse in flavour and may even be enhanced.

A list is given of the main acids found in the popular fruits and it is helpful to add an alternative acid where possible, and if you so wish. But it is perfectly acceptable always to include citric acid when required.

Most fruits contain some acid; some, notably blackcurrants, contain much more than others; some contain hardly any, bananas for example. Cooking varieties of fruits contain more than dessert varieties and unripe or not-quite-ripe fruits contain more than fully ripe fruits.

Flowers, vegetables, herbs, leaves, saps and grains contain either no acid or such a small amount that it can be ignored. For wines made from these ingredients all the acid required must be added.

Finished wines need to contain from five to nine parts acid per thousand of wine depending on the style of wine, its alcohol content and sweetness. A light dry table wine would be well balanced with 5 parts per thousand (ppt), while a very strong and sweet dessert wine would need 8 or 9 ppt. During fermentation some organic acid is converted into other substances, while other acids such as succinic, which contributes to the wine-like smell, are produced. There are no precise measurements yet available and many variable factors seem to be involved. Experiments have shown that musts seemingly low in acid, at around 4 ppt, often finish as wines with around 6 ppt.

Conversely, musts that are initially high in acid produce only another 1 ppt.

When deciding how much acid to add to recipes that you have devised yourself, consideration must be given to the quantity of acid likely to be present in the ingredients. The recipes have all to be calculated with this in mind. A simple test with an acid testing paper will indicate whether the acidity is low, normal or high. The mixing in of some acid and further testing may be necessary. More precise measurement can be made with an acid testing kit which enables you to calculate the quantity of acid present, rather than the degree of acidity. Full details on how to titrate are supplied with the kit and will not be repeated here. The method is quite simple and most people who study chemistry at school are taught how to do this.

In measuring the quantity of acid crystals to add to a must, a simple rule of thumb method is to assume that one level 5 ml spoonful of crystals increases the acid in one gallon of must by one part per thousand. The strained juice of an average sized lemon has the same effect.

Acid is absolutely essential in the making of good wine. It contributes to the bouquet and flavour of the wine, it is needed by the yeast in the process of fermentation, and it helps to protect the wine from deterioration during storage. Low acid wines taste insipid and are prone to a number of infections. Whenever in doubt, add a little more acid rather than a little less. The wine may take longer to mature but will be the better for it.

Tannin This slightly bitter tasting substance is found in the skins of grapes, especially black-skinned grapes, in the skins of pears and in small quantities in other fruits like elderberries. Its presence in a wine contributes to firmness and character. Wines lacking tannin, especially red wines, taste rather soft and flabby. An excess of tannin, especially if it is combined with an excess of acidity, causes astringency; when tasted an astringent wine puckers the gums and cheeks of the mouth. An astringent wine, however, will keep for many years and the excesses will slowly drop out in the form of bottle sediment. Tannin is needed not only for its contribution to the overall flavour of a wine, but also to protect it during maturation. It is best added in the form of a brown and finely powdered grape tannin. One level 5 ml spoonful per gallon is usually enough for red wines, and about half that for whites, especially the hard, dry whites in the Chablis style. Although tannin is present in strong tea, the addition of a cupful or otherwise is not recommended since the quantity of tannin present varies with the brand of tea and the strength of the tea brewed.

Tannin in liquid form is available from some shops, but in use it seems to be less effective than the tannin powder.

Sugar Most fruits contain some fermentable sugars, most vegetables contain very little, and flowers, leaves and grains contain none at all. Vegetables and grains contain starch which can be reduced to sugar with fungal amylase. A yeast, *Saccharomyces distaticus*, can ferment starch to a limited extent. By fermentable sugar in winemaking we mean the fruit sugars, fructose and glucose, and their compound, sucrose, better known as household sugar.

The quantity of sugar present in fruit depends on many factors:

the nature of the fruit for example, dates have a very high sugar content;
the variety culinary varieties usually contain less than dessert varieties;
the ripeness of the fruit under-ripe fruit contains less sugar than fully-ripe fruit;
the season a cold wet summer will produce less sugar in the fruit than a fine and warm summer;
the location some soils are overall more suitable to some fruits or varieties than others.

All of these variables can affect the quantity of sugar present in any sample of fruit. The average quantity present in the more popular fruits has been calculated and the recipes take this into account, but it would be wise to check the quantity with a hydrometer.

When a hydrometer is floated in a strained sample of must, you can read the figure where the level of the sample crosses the chart of the hydrometer. From the tables on page 58 you can see the quantity of sugar represented by this figure that is already present in the must. The actual quantity of household sugar to add to the must depends on this figure. The lower the figure the more sugar is required. The great advantage of knowing this figure is that it enables you to calculate more precisely just how much sugar you need to add to the must to produce the right amount of alcohol for that style of wine.

The cheapest and most suitable sugar to add to a must is granulated household sugar. It can be stirred in, but is sometimes slow to dissolve and needs so much stirring that much air is also admitted – possibly containing spoilage organisms. Another way of adding sugar is to dissolve the quantity required in some boiling water, preferably with a little citric acid, and leave it to cool. The syrup can then be added direct to the must and is readily fermented by the yeast.

Brown sugars contain caramel to a greater or lesser extent and this imparts its flavour to the wine. In some wines this is highly desirable – Madeira-style wines, for example – in others it is a disaster and ruins the wine. This is especially so in white wines and in all lightly flavoured wines.

Fructose and glucose powders are expensive and tend not to be so effective as sucrose which a yeast enzyme can split into the two single sugars. Golden syrup consists of a mixture of sucrose, glucose, fructose and some caramel. Its use in wine-making should be reserved for Madeira-style wines. Cream set honey may be used in moderation, but the honey flavour will be imparted. There is no advantage to be gained from using cube sugar, icing sugar, castor sugar or preserving sugar. They are all more expensive than granulated sugar and in no way superior for wine-making.

Invert sugar is sometimes offered as a superior product for wine-making, but this is not so. In addition to being more expensive than granulated sugar measure for measure, five parts of invert sugar are required for every four parts of granulated sugar. Furthermore, granulated sugar can easily be inverted in the home by boiling it for twenty minutes with a little citric acid. The standard syrup is made from 1 kg/2¼ lb sugar, 5g/1tsp citric acid and 620 ml/1 pint water. The metric formula produces 1.25 litres of syrup, the imperial produces 2 pints. Both have a specific gravity of 1.300.

As well as being aware of the sugar present in the different ingredients, you must also take into account the quantity of alcohol that you want to produce in determining the quantity of sugar to add. Table wines may vary from as little as 9 per cent in some light white wines to as much as 13 per cent in some heavy red wines. In general, it seems best to aim for around 11 per cent for whites and 12 per cent for reds. Social wines are often between 12 and 13 per cent, aperitifs between 13 and 16 per cent and desserts around 16 per cent. Wines to be sparkled should not exceed 11 per cent before refermentation.

Theoretically, if 500 g of sugar is dissolved in water and made up to 5 litres, then almost 6.8 per cent alcohol by volume should be fermented. In practice, this never happens. Some sugar is used by the yeast to provide it with energy, some alcohol is dissipated into the air when the fermenting must is stirred or transferred to another vessel and also in racking. Frequently there is a small residue of sugar when fermentation ends. Yeasts have different conversion rates and some will produce more alcohol than others. The quantity of alcohol present will be marginally diminished in topping up. Calculations made for 4½ litres/1 gallon will be effected if the vessel holds slightly more as many do. Finally, and especially for those who mature their red wines in a cask, some alcohol will evaporate through the staves, particularly if the atmosphere around the cask is humid.

For all these reasons then, the quantity of alcohol to be found in your glass when the wine is poured into it, is likely to be less than you might otherwise have calculated. Professor Fowles of Reading University, who has published much of his research work on different aspects of home wine-making, is of the opinion that in practice we are often lucky to get as much as 6 per cent alcohol from 500 g sugar in 5 litres/1 lb in 1 gallon. In the author's opinion, many people new to wine-making at home will get nearer to 5½ per cent. Taking all these points into consideration, a total of 1 kg/2¼ lb sugar in one standard demijohn of must is enough to produce a dry table wine of about 11 per cent alcohol. The recipes have been formulated on this basis.

Yeast One thing is certain, you cannot make wine without yeast. It was Pasteur who demonstrated this in the mid-nineteenth century. Yeast cells had been seen in fermenting liquids before this, but it was not then known that they caused the conversion of sugar to alcohol and carbon dioxide. The yeast cell is invisible to the naked eye and belongs to the world of botany. Under a powerful microscope the wine yeast cell can be seen to be transparent and elliptical in shape. It measures about $^{7}/_{1000}$ millimetre across. When it is fully grown a bud appears, swells, and eventually splits off from the mother cell which soon starts another bud. Soon, the daughter cell itself produces a bud that swells and splits off. This process takes about three hours in the right conditions and one cell produces some twenty-five to thirty buds during its existence as a viable organism. A sachet of dried yeast granules is likely to contain around a hundred million viable cells which, when activated in a suitable medium, quickly produce thousands of millions of active cells.

Although more than 1,000 different yeasts have been identified, only a few are beneficial in making wine, mead, cider and beer. Yeasts are called saccharomyces, which means sugar fungi, (a mushroom is also a fungus – although a very much larger one). There are many different families and strains of yeast just as there are in vegetables or flowers. (Consider the varieties of the rose with all their strains in different colours and perfumes.) The yeast variety most suitable for wine, mead and cider is *Saccharomyces elipsoideus*, which means eliptical or egg shaped.

The different strains are suitable for different styles of wine, e.g. Sauternes for a full-bodied sweet white wine, Hock for a light white wine, Bordeaux or Burgundy for a dry red table wine, Madeira for a strong caramel-flavour dessert wine, Port for a sweet red dessert wine, Sherry for a strong oxidized aperitif, Champagne for a white sparkling wine and for light flavoured ingredients, such as apples. An all purpose yeast is available for those wines where the flavour of the ingredient is wanted, for example flower wines. A cereal yeast can be used for grain or vegetable wines. This yeast is called *Saccharomyces diastaticus* because it contains the enzyme diastase that converts starch into sugar.

The dried cells are best activated by stirring them into tepid water, i.e. between 40–5°C/104–113°F. At this temperature, the viable cells rehydrate in some fifteen minutes or so. If a little sugar, acid and nutrient is included, the cells will soon start to ferment. The best medium in which to activate dried yeast cells seems to be a dilute solution of grape juice.

Yeast cells need oxygen while they are reproducing themselves, so they should be activated in a bottle that is only a quarter-filled and the neck of which is plugged with cotton wool. It should be frequently shaken to encourage the take-up of oxygen from the air in the bottle.

The yeast cell secretes a number of different enzymes that act as catalysts in causing the conversion of one molecule into another in the chain from the large molecule of fructose or glucose ($C_6H_{12}O_6$) into the smaller molecules of carbon dioxide (CO_2) and ethyl alcohol (C_2H_5OH). On the way, many other substances are produced including other alcohols in minute quantities, some acids and some glycerine.

Some enzymes pass out through the cell wall into the must and reduce the larger molecules of sugar to a size small enough to pass into the cell for reduction by other enzymes. For successful yeast activity it is best to exclude air so that no energy is absorbed in reproduction. Hence the need for the airlock. During the open pulp fermentation some alcohol is formed but not so much as in closed fermentation under an airlock.

Nutrient To remain viable the yeast cells must have ready access to nitrogen and this they obtain from the base ingredients or from the addition of up to 5 g/1 tsp per gallon of must of ammonium phosphate and/or sulphate, more commonly described as yeast nutrient. Vitamin B1 is also needed, and again this is normally available from the base ingredients or by the addition of one 3 mg Benerva tablet per gallon.

The best nutrient, however, is grape in one form or another. It doesn't matter whether you include crushed fresh grapes or pure grape juice bought in a bottle or a waxed carton from the grocer's. Equally suitable is concentrated grape juice, sultanas or raisins. The grape contains not only all the mineral salts, vitamins and trace elements beneficial to fermentation but also a substantial quantity of readily fermentable sugars and valuable tartaric acid. Fresh grapes and grape juice contain around 20 per cent sugar, whilst dried grapes and concentrated grape juice contain around 65 per cent. When including them in a must, allowance must be made for this in the total sugar content. For example, 250 g/9 oz sultanas, or concentrated juice contains just under 170 g/6 oz sugar. Similarly, 1 litre/1¾ pints of pure grape juice would contain about the same quantity.

In addition, these quantities of grape in whatever form, also contribute about, or just over, 1 ppt of acid in one gallon of must.

It is a matter of price and convenience, then, whether you include grapes, grape juice, concentrated grape juice or dried grapes in your must, but experience indicates that it is desirable that you should always include one or the other. The quantity recommended in the recipes is 250 g/9 oz per gallon. The figure is by no means critical, however, and some very competent wine-makers use only two-thirds or even half the figure recommended.

If you decide to use 1 litre/1¾ pints of pure grape juice instead of 250 g/9 oz of sultanas, however, do remember to use less water than indicated. Indeed, if you vary the recipes in any way, and there is no reason why you should not, then you must remember to adjust other components accordingly.

The practice of wine-making

The making of wine can be divided into three stages: preparation, fermentation and maturation.

Preparation includes all the activities up to the addition of the yeast.

Fermentation begins with the addition of the activated yeast and continues until the young wine is ready for removal from its sediment.

Maturation begins with this first racking and continues until the wine is ready for drinking.

Preparation

Fruits

The basic ingredients should always be of the finest quality obtainable. Poor quality ingredients will produce poor wine and be a waste of time and money. This is not to say that bruised or damaged fruits should never be used. They may be used, but only after the bruised or damaged portions have been cut out and discarded. The remaining portions will then, no doubt, be of good quality.

All fruits should have their stalks removed and discarded, for these impart a bitter taste to the wine. The fruit should then be washed in running cold water to remove any leaves, insects, dust, etc. Fruits containing stones should be cut open and the stone removed and discarded. Failure to do this will also cause an unpleasant taste in the wine. The fruit should then be liquidized, crushed or cut up into small pieces as may be most convenient to you, so that the juice containing the sugars, acids, tannins, colour, minerals, vitamins, etc. can be extracted.

The colour from crushed red fruits can best be extracted by pouring hot water over them, and allowing them to soak under cover until cool. A pectic enzyme should then be added to break down the pectin (the setting factor in jam) and so ensure the maximum juice extraction as well as the avoidance of a pectin haze in the finished wine. Pectic enzyme works best in the absence of too much sugar and so it is common practice also to add one crushed Campden tablet per gallon together with any additional acid required. This protects the must from infection during the following twenty-four hours while the enzyme activity is taking place and before the yeast is added.

White and rosé fruits make better wine when cold water is added instead of hot. The pectic enzyme, acid and sulphite should be added as for red wine. The quantity of pectic enzyme to add varies from one manufacturer to another. Generally, one level teaspoonful of liquid, or one rounded teaspoonful of white powder, is sufficient in one gallon. Some fruits, especially those that make jam easily, need a somewhat larger quantity. Wines made from jam require at least a double dose. The enzyme works best in a temperature around 27°C/80°F, if this can be arranged.

After the pectic enzyme has been at work for twenty-four hours, the must should be stirred well and a quantity removed, gently pressed and strained into a trial jar so that a hydrometer reading can be made. In addition to the sugar, the must will contain a number of other ingredients including some particles of fruit pulp. In calculating the sugar content, it would be wise to reduce the reading by, say, four points, thus making an allowance for the other items.

Fruit juices merely have to be emptied from their cartons, cans or bottles into a demijohn. The juices usually contain some pectin, and so it would be sensible to add some pectic enzyme.

Dried fruits should be washed in warm water to remove dust, dirt and oil. Some fruits, especially sultanas and raisins, are sprayed with medicinal liquid paraffin to make them shiny and attractive and to prevent them sticking together in clumps. Whilst this oil is not injurious it can inhibit fermentation and so is best removed. Sultanas and raisins can then be chopped up and added to the must. Larger dried fruits, such as prunes, figs and apricots, should be steeped in hot water overnight to rehydrate them. The prune stones can then be removed and the flesh crushed and chopped; similarly with the apricots and figs. Always include in the must the water in which the fruit was steeped since it will contain some sugar and other required ingredients.

Canned fruits should be strained from their syrup which should then be saved. Any stones should be removed, the fruit crushed, water poured over them, pectic enzyme, acid and sulphite added, then treated as fresh fruit. The syrup should be added just prior to the hydrometer check.

Frozen fruits should be thawed in a sulphite solution to prevent the oxidation of any broken or damaged fruits. If the fruit is just taken

Average sugar content of popular fruits

	454 g in 4.54 litres	*1 lb in 1 gallon*
dates, raisins and sultanas	300 g	10½ oz
grapes	70–100 g	2½–3½ oz
bananas	80 g	3 oz
apples, cherries, elderberries, greengages, oranges, pears, peaches	40–50 g	1½–2 oz
apricots, bilberries, blackberries, blackcurrants, damsons, loganberries, mulberries, plums, raspberries, redcurrants, strawberries	20–40 g	¾–1½ oz
gooseberries, grapefruit, lemons, rhubarb	5–20 g	¼–¾ oz

from the freezer and allowed to thaw in a warm room it can quickly deteriorate. It is better to put it straight into a must and to crush when thawed by squeezing it in clean hands. Fruits otherwise difficult to

Average acidity of popular fruits

	dominant acid	*degree*	*ppt**
blackcurrant	citric	very high	2.5
red and white currant	citric		
damson	malic		
lemon	citric		
cherry (cooking)	malic	high to very high	2.0
gooseberry	citric/malic		
greengage	malic		
rhubarb	malic		
apricot	malic	high	1.5
plum	malic		
raspberry	citric		
apple (cooking)	malic	medium to high	1.2
blackberry	citric/malic		
grape	tartaric		
pineapple	citric		
quince	malic		
strawberry	citric		
elderberry	citric	medium	1
orange	citric		
apple (eating)	malic	low to medium	0.7
bilberry	citric		
cherry (eating)	malic		
mulberry	citric		
peach	malic		
raisins and sultanas	tartaric		
banana	malic	very low	less than 0.5
pear	malic		
fig	citric		
date	citric		

*454 g/1 lb fruit in 4.54 litres/1 gallon.

crush usually soften easily after having been frozen and then thawed.

Fruits make wines of all kinds, but it is sensible to be aware of their different attributes when deciding what style of wine to make from a particular fruit. The stronger the flavour of the fruit, the more suitable it is for a dessert wine. Lighter flavoured fruits should be used for table wines. Some fruits like bananas, dates, figs and prunes, are best used with other ingredients. Highly acidic fruits, like rhubarb, lemons and blackcurrants, tend not to make a good wine unless blended with less acid ingredients.

Vegetables

Only a few vegetables are really worth using for wine – beetroot, carrot, parsnip and potato – and the last-named is best used with other ingredients. They are all best made into dessert wines. Use new season vegetables, freshly dug, washed clean from every trace of earth, trimmed, chopped and boiled until soft but not mushy. Strain out the vegetables and use only the liquor for making the wine. Onions and salads are not suitable, nor brassicas.

Beetroot and carrot juices can be bought from some health food shops and may be used for making wine. Similarly, fresh vegetables may be liquidized and the juice alone used for the must. In these circumstances it is only necessary to dilute the juice, add pectic enzyme, acid and sulphite, leave it under cover for twenty-four hours, then add sugar, nutrient and yeast.

Flowers, leaves and herbs

The only contribution that these ingredients have to offer is bouquet and flavour. Everything else that makes wine must be added. The old country method was merely to add lemon juice, sugar and yeast. A modern method is to use them to flavour diluted grape juice concentrate.

The flowers should be picked when they are fully opened, preferably in the middle of a sunny morning after the dew has evaporated, but before the perfume has dissipated. Collect them in a basket or paper bag. Try not to use a polythene bag since this causes condensation in the bag and makes the petals damp.

Remove all leaves, stalks and calyx since these impart an unpleasant bitterness to the wine. Use only the fragrant petals. The stronger the perfume, the fewer flowers should be used. Traditionally, they are measured by volume. Place them in a half-pint mug, for example, and shake them down by gently banging the mug a few times on a work surface. Do not press them down.

Dried flowers from herbalists and health food shops may be used instead of fresh flowers. A small 50 g/2 oz packet is sufficient to flavour 4½ litres/1 gallon of wine. The essential flavouring substances from flowers are best obtained by pouring hot water over them and rubbing the petals against a hard surface such as a ceramic bowl, with the back of a strong plastic or wooden spoon. This should be done several times over a couple of days. In between macerating the container should be kept closely covered. When the water is cool, it should be further protected with one level teaspoonful citric acid and one crushed Campden tablet per gallon. Finally, strain out, press dry and discard the petals, and use only the liquor for making the wine. The addition of a container of concentrated grape juice and a yeast would be sufficient to make an attractive wine.

Flowers are, perhaps, best used not to make an exclusively flower flavoured wine but added in small quantities to other wines to enhance their bouquet. They are especially beneficial when using ingredients with little flavouring of their own. This is equally true of certain leaves, blackcurrant, blackberry, oak, walnut and vines, for example. The leaves should be just mature but still young and tender and free from marks of any kind that imply infection from fungi. Also, the leaves should not have been sprayed with any bactericidal or fungicidal mixture. Wash them thoroughly just to make sure. Chop them up and boil them to extract the constituent juices. Alternatively, these ingredients may be frozen and when thawed rubbed into fragments that can be added to fruit musts. Blackcurrant, vine, blackberry and oak leaves are particularly suitable as flavour additives to 'red' musts.

Herbs are usually extremely bitter or possessed of such a strong flavour that they need to be used with great care. Parsley is perhaps the exception. Other herbs again, like flowers and leaves, are best used in small quantities to provide a subtle and complex bouquet to a wine made from some other base ingredient. Similarly, with spices; ginger alone makes an acceptable distinctive flavouring to a wine. Others, such as cloves and cinnamon, are best used in moderation to flavour wines made from marrows or melons. Crush the spices with a rolling pin, place them in a net bag and suspend them in a fermenting must for two or three days until you have extracted sufficient flavour for your palate; but go easy.

Grains

Although sometimes used when no other ingredient is available, cereals are not really suitable for making wine. Wholemeal rice is sometimes used with raisins, and wheat has also been used. Barley is best used to make wine in the form of a strong beer; maize, oats and rye have nothing to offer the wine-maker worth the time, trouble and money involved.

Wheat and rice should be crushed or coarsely ground. If you grind too finely you will just make a gooey paste. All that is needed is to open the husk. Often this can best be done by washing the grains in running water to remove the dust and then softening them by a soaking in hot water for about an hour. A rolling pin and a formica-type surface may then be sufficient to break them open. A second or two in a liquidizer is an alternative.

Pour boiling water over the grains and, when cool, add the other ingredients to make the wine. The cereal contributes a little flavour, some gluten that gives body, and some starch. It is as essential to add fungal amylase to a cereal wine as it is to add pectic enzyme to a fruit wine. Otherwise you will have a starch haze in your wine. All the acid required must be added but there is plenty of nitrogen in grains. It is better to ferment grain wines with *Saccharomyces distaticus* rather than *Saccharomyces ellipsoideus*, the wine yeast. *S.distaticus* is able to ferment starch to a limited extent. If grains are used they make a better dessert wine than a table wine. Their best use – again if used at all – is in combination with other ingredients, for example, potatoes.

Fermentation

Yeast, and the enzymes which it secretes, is the cause of fermentation and is readily available to the home wine-maker. It can be bought in a sealed polythene-lined foil sachet containing not only some dried and granulated yeast but also a few grains of nutrient salts and sugar. It can also be bought as a compressed yeast tablet, again sealed in a foil sachet. Members of wine-making circles are also

able to buy fine quality wine yeasts dried and granulated an
in a sealed, double layer polythene sachet.

Activating the yeast

The yeast may be added to the must simply by shaking the loose contents of the sachets, or crumbling the tablet, over the must. Eventually the yeast will rehydrate and begin fermentation. It is more effective, however, if the granules are first activated in half a cup of tepid water (40–45°C/104–113°F) for fifteen minutes or in an equally tepid dilute solution of concentrated grape juice. When this is added to the must, the already activated yeast cells are able to begin the fermentation of the sugar without delay.

While the yeast is being activated it is a good idea to check that the must contains sufficient acid, nitrogen, phosphorous, potassium and other trace elements. Most fruits contain these substances although not always in adequate quantities. Grapes contain them all hence the desirability of always including some in the must. Yeast nutrient crystals always include diammonium phosphate. Vitamin B1 is also a desirable element again available in the grape.

Temperatures

The temperature of the must should now be checked. Yeast ferments best within the range 19–24°C/66–75°F, although it will ferment within the wider range of 15°C/59°F to 30°C/86°F. At the extremes of this range fermentation is sluggish and can become stuck, i.e. activity will cease. Normally when the temperature increases or decreases towards the middle range activity will resume. The actual fermentation releases some heat. In a 4½ litre/1 gallon jar it may be no more than 1 or 2°F, but in a 45 or 90 litre/10 or 20 gallon container it would be as much as 3 or 4°F.

At the outset of the fermentation it is as well to have a temperature of around 21°C/70°F, and this temperature may be maintained for red wines. Experience shows, however, that white wines develop a better bouquet and flavour if they can be fermented at a slightly lower temperature, around 17°C/63°F, or even a degree or two lower if the temperature can be maintained without fluctuations. To this end, you may find it helpful to cover your fermentation vessel with some kind of lagging; for example a cardboard carton in which the container fits snugly, several layers of newspaper, a thick towel or piece of blanket, or insulated wrapping of some other kind.

Fermenting on the pulp

When the yeast starts to ferment, activity is sometimes tumultuous. Great frothing may occur and musts in a jar may even boil over and make a mess. The verb to ferment comes from the French word *fervere* which means to boil. The frothing can be contained in the jar by leaving a good airspace and only plugging the neck with cotton wool. Particles of fruit pulp are lifted up by the carbon dioxide and when they are expelled from the jar they leave a sticky trail down the side of the jar on to the surface beneath. Apart from the mess, the deposit becomes an attraction for all kinds of spoilage organisms. Should a must 'boil over', the mess should be wiped off as soon as possible with a cloth that has been dampened with a sulphite solution.

When crushed fruits are being fermented on the pulp, the carbon dioxide lifts up the fruit above the surface of the liquid. In this position it forms an ideal breeding ground for spoilage organisms, notably *Mycoderma aceti*, the vinegar bug. Furthermore, the essential constituents of colour, sugar and acid, etc. cannot be extracted. The cap must, therefore, be kept submerged either by a china plate, weighted if necessary, or by gently pressing down the cap and mixing it into the liquid at least twice a day. In between, the container should be kept loosely covered with a lid or a thick cloth.

Fermentation on the pulp should not be allowed to continue for more than a few days, since too much bitterness will result. The one exception is when wine is being made exclusively from black grapes, or from sultanas or raisins. Fermentation may then be allowed to continue for about ten days.

During pulp fermentation only a few degrees of alcohol are formed, partly because the must does not, and should not, contain too much sugar – except for grape wine – and partly because the yeast continues to reproduce itself in the presence of the oxygen in the liquid and the air as the pulp cap is pressed down. But the alcohol as it is formed does help in the extraction of the constituent parts of the fruit. The constant movement caused by rising bubbles of carbon dioxide also helps.

Straining and pressing

When the period of pulp fermentation is over, the solid particles must be removed. This is best done by straining the entire must through a fine mesh nylon straining bag and gently pressing it until all the liquid has been removed. If the pulp is very mushy, it may be sufficient just to drain the pulp in a nylon strainer, or to roll it gently in a straining bag without pressing it at all. It is undesirable to carry over a lot of fine particles of pulp.

With firmer or larger fruits, such as apples, the pulp should be pressed hard and frequently stirred up to ensure the maximum extraction of juice. A wine press is of great assistance in these circumstances.

Adding sugar

Additional sugar should now be mixed into the liquid must. Adding sugar granules in their dry state causes much foaming. If this is how you propose to add your sugar, leave the must in a bin while the sugar is stirred in so that the foaming is well contained in the bin. Even if the sugar is to be added in the form of syrup, it should be poured in slowly and gently stirred. The must should then be poured through a large funnel into a demijohn and, if all the sugar required has been added, the jar should be topped up with cold boiled water. An airlock already fitted into a bored bung should then be filled with a sulphite solution and the bung should be gently pushed into the neck of the jar with a screwing action. It is important to effect a good seal between the inlet tube of the airlock and the bung, and between the bung and the neck of the jar. Otherwise the carbon dioxide will escape without passing through the airlock and you may think that fermentation has stopped.

When you are making high alcohol wines, it is more effective in reaching the maximum quantity of alcohol if you add the sugar in several portions, and not all at once. In this way, you gradually build up the alcohol tolerance of the yeast. Some yeasts, such as Tokay, Madeira, Port and Sherry, have a higher tolerance than yeast such as Hock. By fermenting with a suitable yeast, well fortified with nutrients, vitamins and the various trace elements, a must can be encouraged with several doses of sugar to produce as much as 16 or occasionally 17 per cent alcohol.

Care should be taken not to stir the must too much so as not to dissipate any alcohol. In making strong wines it really is best to add sugar only in the form of syrup. It is only necessary to remove the airlock bung, pour in a measure of syrup and replace the bung without further disturbance of the must. If the sugar is used dry some must has to be removed from the jar, the sugar stirred in until dissolved, and the must poured back. This involves far too much stirring and the admission of additional oxygen as well as the loss of alcohol. With the oxygen the yeast starts reproducing itself again instead of fermenting, and activity may cease for a while.

If you wish to make a strong dry wine, you must watch the specific gravity of the must as you get towards a high alcohol. Sometimes a hydrometer can be floated in the must and left in the jar throughout the fermentation. If you can do this you need not add the second dose of sugar until the reading is down to 1.002. The reading will immediately increase and then begin to fall as that sugar is fermented. Subsequent doses should be very small. Just enough to keep the fermentation going. With care, it is possible to produce quite strong dry wines in this manner.

Stuck ferments Occasionally a must will stop fermenting before you think that it should. The first action to take is to check the specific gravity. Not infrequently all the sugar is converted within a few days and the fermentation is finished. If the reading is high, however, it may be that the fermentation has stopped temporarily because of too low or too high a temperature, as already mentioned. The remedy is to move the must to a warmer or cooler place whichever is necessary. In very hot weather a jar can be placed in a bowl of cold water and covered with cloths, the ends of which dip into the water.

If temperature is not the cause, the must may have become clogged with carbon dioxide. It is worth pouring the must through a funnel into another jar, making as much splash as possible. This not only dissipates the carbon dioxide (and some alcohol) but also admits some air which will enable the yeast to reproduce itself and restart the fermentation.

It may also be that the yeast has insufficient nutrient, vitamin B1 or acid. Always check that you have included sufficient of these in one form or another in your must. Sometimes it is possible to mix in these ingredients at a later time, but all too often the yeast has died off by then and this late addition has no effect.

Another reason for a stuck ferment is the addition of too much sugar too soon. If the must contains too much sugar, the density of the must liquid may well be greater than the density of the liquid inside the yeast cell. As a result, it will not be possible for the molecules and enzymes to pass to and fro through the cell wall. In extreme circumstances, the cell liquid may pass out into the must to maintain an equilibrium, the cell wall will then cave in and the yeast will die.

If the yeast has died the only way to reactivate the ferment is with an entirely new yeast regenerated in a starter bottle. As soon as it is fermenting well add to it an equal quantity of the stuck must. When that is fermenting add another equal quantity. So, if the starter consists of 500 ml, then add 500 ml of stuck must, when that is working add one litre, when that is working add two litres and when that is working add the remainder. It is almost always a waste of yeast and effort to add a yeast direct to the stuck must.

As fermentation nears completion, the number of tiny bubbles rising in the must diminishes and the much larger bubbles passing through the airlock become slower and ever more infrequent. When all activity ceases, the wine begins to clear at the neck of the jar and a deposit starts to build up on the bottom. This is the time to remove the wine from its sediment and let it start on the sometimes painfully slow path to maturation.

Maturation

Although the wine should be removed as soon as possible from its sediment, it will come to no harm if it is first left for a few days in a cold place. The reduction in the thermal currents and the lower temperature assist the particles to settle down firmly on the bottom of the jar. This not only makes racking easier but also removes more particles first time round.

Racking Racking the clear wine from its sediment is one of the oldest activities in wine-making. Nowadays, it is best performed with the aid of a siphon. The jar of wine should be placed on a work surface and the receiving jar on the floor or a low stool beneath. After removing the airlock and bung and inserting the entry end of the siphon into the wine, suck the outflow end until the tube is full, squeeze this end, place it at once in the receiving jar and release the pressure. It is much easier if you can turn a tiny tap off and on. Let the wine flow steadily down the side of the jar, and as soon as there is sufficient wine in the jar to cover the tap or outflow, submerge it so that there is no splashing and the admission of air is reduced to the minimum. If you can leave the wine to flow by itself for a moment or two, add 5 ml/1 tsp of a 10 per cent solution of sulphite or one crushed Campden tablet per gallon. This will prevent excessive oxidation of the wine and inhibit the development of spoilage organisms.

As the wine in the jar above gradually nears the sediment, you can slowly and carefully tilt the jar, whilst keeping firm control over the entry tube. Always keep the orifice of the tube above the sediment and ensure that no sediment is picked up by the suction and carried over. With practice and care very little wine need be wasted. If through some misfortune the last of the wine gets mixed up with the sediment, transfer it to a suitably sized bottle, seal it and leave it in a cold place for a few days while it clears, then remove the clear wine.

Topping up If the receiving jar is not quite full, it must be topped up to the neck with wine of a similar kind, or with cold boiled water. Alternatively, sterilized glass marbles or small pebbles may be used to make up the volume. Seal the jar with a softened bung pushed well home. A piece of string or plastic-covered wire, inserted into the neck of the jar before the bung is pushed home and subsequently removed, ensures a perfect seal. Label the jar with its name and dates, etc. and store it in a cool dark place until it is clear or until further deposit has been thrown. Rack the wine again not later than six weeks after the first racking and top it up as before.

Fining If the wine is not clearing, finings may be added in accordance with the manufacturer's instructions. Bentonite is the most widely used fining agent at present. It is available both as a gel and as soluble granules. Avoid buying the grey powder because it is very difficult to disseminate in the wine. There are a number of excellent proprietary brands of fining agents available, usually in a gel form. You simply mix the appropriate quantity of gel into 250 ml/½ pint of wine and then mix that into the rest of the gallon.

After fining a wine, it should be left in the coldest place you can find for about a week by which time it will usually be clear. If it is not, then the cause of the haze is likely to be pectin if it is a fruit wine, or starch if it is a vegetable or cereal wine. A pectin haze can be determined by mixing 5 ml/1 teaspoonful of the wine into 20 ml of methylated spirits. Shake it very well, then leave it for a while. If the cause is pectin, then small dots or threads will appear in the liquid. The remedy is to add a strong dose of a pectic enzyme to the wine and leave it in a warm place,

21°C/70°F for a day or two, then in a cold place for a week, by which time the wine will be clear and ready for racking again.

Starch hazes are fairly rare. The test is to place 15 ml of wine in the centre of a white saucer and then add two or three drops of household iodine from the first aid kit. If starch is present, the wine will turn blue or darken. Dark red wines may have to be diluted so that any change can be seen. The remedy is a dose of fungal amylase, well mixed in and left for a week to clear.

Plum wines often develop a 'bloom' during maturation. It looks like a very faint haze but is not moved by any fining agent. The cause is thought to be the hydrophylic wax on the skin of the plums. When wine is being made from plums, it is recommended that they first be washed in hot water containing a little washing soda and then rinsed in cold running water. This usually prevents the development of this problem.

Filtering After fining a wine it may be necessary to filter it. Indeed some wine-makers filter their wines as a matter of course soon after the first racking. These wine-makers also often add bentonite with the yeast so that the wine will clear more quickly when fermentation is finished. The belief is that wines mature best in the absence of unwanted debris of every kind.

Storage Wines usually mature more quickly and more effectively in bulk than in bottle, although fast maturing light white wines are best bottled as soon as they are clear. They can then develop their bouquet and flavour in the bottle without the disturbance of bottling after a period of maturation in bulk. Heavier red table wines and strong dessert wines, however, need at least one year, and often longer, in bulk, followed by a further period in bottle. At all times keep the wine shielded from light and in a cool and even temperature, 10–15°C/50–59°F is best.

Bungs on jars should be checked from time to time in case they have become loose. Bottles should be filled to within 2 cm/1 inch of the bottom of the cork and stored on their sides. This keeps the cork moist and therefore swollen and tight, and leaves a bubble of air over the centre of the body of the wine to provide sufficient oxygen for the maturation process.

Frequently, a further deposit is formed on the bottom side of the bottle during long storage. Before serving such a wine, the bottle should be stood up for a few days so that the sediment can settle in the punt of the bottle. The clear wine can then be poured or siphoned into a decanter leaving the sediment behind.

Blending No matter how carefully you follow recipes and make your wines, you will find that some please you more than others. Do not despair of the others. They would probably improve if left to mature longer. They will certainly improve if you blend them.

When you feel that the wines are sufficiently mature, bring them out of store and taste them. If they please you as they are, then bottle them. But some may taste too sweet or too sharp, or too thin or too bland. If you have followed the advice in this book, none of them should have bacterial faults, but ingredients vary enormously and inevitably some wines do not turn out as hoped for. This is equally true of commercial wines.

As long as the wines smell and taste clean and free from off odours and flavours, they may be blended. Blending improves wines in quite extraordinary ways not yet fully understood. The individual wines seem to contribute only their good qualities and lose their less pleasant. But blending is an art rather than a science. It is not very helpful to mix small quantities into cocktails, adding a little drop more of one and a little less of another until you have a pleasant taste in the glass. In time the wines will homogenize and the taste may then change considerably.

It seems better to consider each wine separately, noting its good and bad points and their degree as best you can. Then decide how to blend the wines together. As a rule of thumb, mix opposites together, but don't be afraid to mix a really dark red wine with a white wine. Indeed, depending on the depth of the red or the proportion of the red to white, this may be a good way of making an attractive rosé, or conversely of 'stretching' the red! These practices are well known in commercial circles.

Siphon the wines from their containers into a larger and freshly sterilized bin, give them a gentle stir to mix them thoroughly, then siphon the blended wine back into freshly washed and sterilized containers. Fit airlocks to the jars, for sometimes new fermentations occur. If you are blending all white, add one Campden tablet, or its equivalent, per gallon to prevent infection and oxidation. It is better not to sulphite red wines in case a *malo-lactic fermentation* is prevented.

Many red wines benefit from a hint of blackcurrant aroma and flavour. At this stage you could consider mixing in a tablespoonful or two of a concentrated blackcurrant juice, such as Ribena. This is an occasion where tasting and increasing the additive is important. Always add too little at first. You can always add a little more, but it is impossible to remove too much.

Dessert wines in the port style may benefit from a dose of vodka or even a few drops of capsicum tincture. This imparts a warm glow to the wine. Capsicum tincture can be bought for a few pence from most chemists if you explain what you want it for. Chemists stock it in bulk for use in making up prescriptions and will usually sell it in 20 ml quantities if asked to do so.

Dessert wines also need richness and if this is lacking a tablespoonful or two of glycerine per gallon may be the answer. It is certainly worth trying, for it can make an enormous difference to a wine. Too many sweet wines lack the body and richness needed to lift them out of the rut of the ordinary. It is these touches of Ribena, vodka, capsicum tincture and glycerine, not to mention the odd bottle of commercial wine, that enables some wine-makers to produce so much better wines than others. What matters is the final taste of the wine in your mouth.

Blended wines need at least a month to homogenize, often a further deposit is thrown. The next problem is to think of a new name for them.

Special wine types

The information so far given has been for the preparation, fermentation and maturation of table wines. In many ways much of this advice applies to the making of all wines, but there are some variations to be observed in the making of sparkling wines and sherry style wines in particular.

A better wine can be made with certain ingredients than with others. For example, elderberries make a better, rich, well flavoured dessert wine than they do a sparkling or sherry style wine. The recipes give examples of the different ingredients that experience has shown to be more suitable than others for these purposes. This does not exclude sensible experimentation, but rather points the way to explore.

Sparkling wines

Sparkling wine seems best made from lightly flavoured ingredients, not used in excessive quantities, nor too strong in alcohol. Since it is the very essence of a sparkling wine to be fermented a second time, it is essential that so much alcohol is not produced in the first fermentation that it inhibits the second. A careful control of the *total* sugar content of the must is necessary since all the sugar must be fermented and a very dry base wine produced. It is advisable to keep this total sugar content below 880 g/31 oz per gallon.

To ensure the complete fermentation of this quantity of sugar, sufficient nutrient must be included, especially some grape with its many trace elements. Ferment at as low a temperature as you can with a champagne wine yeast to develop the best flavour, free from the coarseness that sometimes comes from a fermentation at a high temperature.

When fermentation is finished rack and, if necessary, filter the wine, although this is best avoided if the wine can be cleared naturally. The wine should be stored in a full and well-sealed demijohn, in a cool dark place, for a minimum of six months before it is re-fermented.

Second fermentation At this time bring the jar to a warmer place and, provided there is no sediment in the jar, the next stage can begin. If there is any sediment, then siphon the wine into another demijohn and check the specific gravity to make sure that is below 0.996. Then mix in 70g/2½oz sugar per gallon. This is one of the few precise figures in wine-making. If you cannot weigh this quantity with some degree of accuracy, then use fifteen level 5ml teaspoonsful. Use the back of a knife to ensure that each spoonful is level.

Remove half a cupful or so of the wine, warm it slightly to 40°C/104°F, stir in the sugar and, when it is dissolved, add a second champagne wine yeast with just a pinch more nutrient. After fifteen minutes, return this to the jar, fit an airlock and leave it in a warm place for a few hours.

Meanwhile, sterilize six proper champagne bottles and hollow-domed plastic stoppers; then prepare six wire cages and labels giving details of the ingredients of the wine, the date it was started and the date it was re-fermented.

Bottling As soon as fermentation is renewed in the jar, siphon the wine into the champagne bottles and fill each one to within 5 cm/2 in of the top. This airspace is needed to contain the pressure of the gas that will be formed, so be careful not to overfill the bottles. Push home the plastic stoppers with the heel of your hand and wire on the cages. It is easier to get a flush fit if the stoppers are first softened in hot water. Do not hit them with a mallet or hammer since this would damage the dome. In fitting the cages, ensure that the bottom wire is securely fixed beneath the lip of the bottle and twisted tightly. There will be great pressure on the stopper and it must not be allowed to rise. Now stick on the labels and lay the bottles on their side in a warm place for three or four days while the sugar is fermented. Fermentation is more successful when the bottles are lying down.

Maturation The bottles must next be moved to a cold dark store and left undisturbed, again for a minimum of six months. Once more, it is necessary to lay the bottles on their side so that the special flavour of the champagne yeast can develop. Keep the labels uppermost and cover them with tissue to keep them clean.

When next you examine the bottles you should see a thin layer of sediment, sometimes in the shape of a feather, all the way down the bottom side of the bottle. The time has come to remove this. A simple way to do this in the home is to place the bottles head down in a bottle carton and to prop the carton at an angle of 45° so that the sediment can slide down into the hollow stopper. It has to be encouraged to do this, and each day, each bottle should be given a gentle shake and twist over a period of three or four weeks until it can be seen that the sides of the bottle are absolutely clean and the sediment is all in the neck. Now stand the bottles completely on their stoppers and encourage the sediment into them, so that when the stoppers are removed the sediment comes too.

Disgorging the sediment Stand the bottles, still upside down, in a cold refrigerator overnight, then crush a trayful of ice and mix with it two tablespoonsful of cooking salt. Place this in a basin and stand the bottles, one at a time, in the mixture so the stopper and neck of the bottle are covered. Within ten minutes the wine in the stopper will be frozen and the sediment encapsulated.

Soften some more stoppers in hot water and lay out on a saucer some saccharin pellets. These are needed to soften and smooth the very dry edge of the wine.

When the stopper is frozen, gently right the bottle, undo the wire cage and take it off. Then, with the aid of a cloth twist out the stopper, pop in one, two or three saccharin pellets, depending on how sweet you want the finished wine, fit a clean stopper and wire on the cage. With thoughtful preparation the process of removing one stopper and fitting the other takes no more than a second or two, especially if someone else is available to pop in the saccharin pellets.

If the wine has been well chilled and the gas has not been shaken loose by careless handling, there will be no foaming, provided no more than the precise amount of sugar was added to a completely dry wine.

The sparkling wine is now finished and ready for serving, but will remain in excellent condition for many months.

Serving When a bottle is to be opened and served, have sufficient tall fluted glasses available, together with a large jug. Remove the wire cage, ease out the stopper and allow the first foaming to flow into the jug, rather than to overflow a glass. The wine can then be poured slowly down the side of a tilted glass until it is two-thirds full. Only a little frothing should occur but several strong beads of bubbles should be seen rising in the glass. They should continue for a quarter of an hour or so. If the bottle is not emptied, replace the stopper without delay and a second round can subsequently be poured with equal success. The foaming that went into the jug will quickly settle down and should be returned to the bottle.

Sparkling wines are not difficult to make successfully if the directions given above are followed. On special occasions, there is no wine comparable with a sparkling wine. To have made it yourself doubles the pleasure.

Sherry style wines

These, too, can be equally successful if similar thought and care is given to their making. Sadly, they take longer to mature. Again, use sensible ingredients, with sufficient acid and plenty of nutrient. A high alcohol wine is required so the total sugar content can be as high as 1.36 kg/3 lb per gallon, provided it is mixed in a little at a time.

Rosehips and figs, parsnips and figs, Seville oranges, prunes, Victoria plums, dates and rhubarb all make interesting sherry style wines, especially with the aid of some kind of grapes. Follow the method of prolonged fermentation described on page 51, but when the wine has finished fermenting and been racked from its sediment, leave it to mature in jars only half to three quarters full, the necks being plugged with cotton wool rather than bungs.

Rack the wine frequently, not only to remove the sediment, but also to oxidize the wine. Usually two years or longer is necessary to mature the wine and develop a good flavour. The latter can be enhanced if one gallon of sherry style wine is racked from its lees after fermentation into two demijohns, half filling each. Then pour half a bottle of a commercial sherry of similar style, i.e. dry, medium or sweet, into each jar. Over the period of maturation the older wine imparts its flavour to the younger wine.

Sherry is a blended wine and this can be emulated in the home by making up, say, three wines, from different ingredients. Blend these into an 'ex-sherry five'. This is a plastic cube in a cardboard carton and used by restaurants and hotels selling large quantities of sherry by the glass. The plastic cube is fitted with a cap containing a tap. While the wines are maturing, leave the cask on its back with the tap uppermost and open, although lightly plugged with cotton wool. This filters out the spoilage organisms in the air but permits the passage of air in and out of the cask as the wine contracts and expands with seasonal temperature variations.

When the wine is sufficiently mature, close the tap, revert the box to its proper position, leave it for a week to settle, then draw off, say, six bottles full. Turn the box back to its former position, remove the cap from the cube and mix in another gallon of sherry style wine that has already achieved some maturity. Replace the cap, open the tap, plug it lightly, and leave it until a further supply is needed. In this way, you can build up quite a useful solera system not that dissimilar to the commercial system.

If you can obtain a small sherry cask – they sometimes come in a 30-litre/6½-gallon size – so much the better. The bung hole is in an end stave and the tap in the far end of a side stave. The cask is stood upright and not on its side, but needs to be kept at least two-thirds full. The major difficulty in making sherry style wines is the time they take to mature and homogenize after blending. They improve so much with age.

Madeira style wines

The golden sponge cake that was invented during the reign of Queen Victoria to accompany these noble wines is, like the wines, still available although less in demand than then. The increasing popularity of the island of Madeira for holidays, however, is widening the number of people who have tasted and enjoyed Madeira wines. Home wine-makers are now looking for ways to make similar wines at a fraction of the cost.

Madeira is, in fact, four different wines: Sercial, the driest; Verdelho, the semi-dry; Boal, the sweet; and Malmsey the rich and luscious dessert wine.

Again, thought must be given to the basic ingredients. Rose hips and raisins spring to mind for Malmsey, but also use brown sugar rather than white; it enhances the caramel flavour. Dried apricots, some concentrated white grape juice and a little honey will produce a Sercial style. Remember to include sufficient acid and nutrient, but raisins are by far the best nutrient.

Always use a Madeira yeast and ferment the must with added brown sugar to maximize alcohol content. When the wine is finished and clear, mature it in the warmest place you can find for three to six months. An atmospheric temperature of between 50–60°C/122–140°F is about right. The Malmsey style wine should be finished sweet with a specific gravity between 1.020 and 1.030. And 28 ml/1 fl oz of glycerine to the finished wine to enhance the smooth and silky texture.

This wine also benefits by being heavily oxidized and the best results will be obtained by maturing one gallon of wine with a bottle of Malmsey in two demijohns. The necks of the jars should be plugged with cotton wool, especially during the period of warm storage.

If possible, 56 ml/2 fl oz of Polish spirit should be added after the period of hot maturation to make up for any alcohol lost by dissipation. The contents of the two jars may then be combined and stored under a bung for several years before serving.

Madeira wines need very long storage and will keep for a great many years, improving for most of that time.

They make a splendid accompaniment to a piece of Madeira cake at any time of the day.

Fortified wines

With the inclusion of sufficient acid, nutrient and vitamin B1, the control of an even temperature and the continued addition of small quantities of sugar over a period of weeks, certain yeasts will produce a very high level of alcohol and quite enough for most aperitif and dessert wines. There are occasions, however, when it is desirable to fortify a wine with additional alcohol. For the best results always use vodka which is both colourless and tasteless, or Polish spirit which is twice as strong and, therefore, only half as much is required. This also minimizes the dilution of the flavour of the wine.

Before beginning to fortify a wine, its alcohol content should be known and the alcohol level required should be determined. It is then a simple calculation to find out how much spirit is needed.

Draw a square and write the letters A and B in the top left and right hand corners, and D and E in the bottom left and right hand corners. In the centre write the letter C.

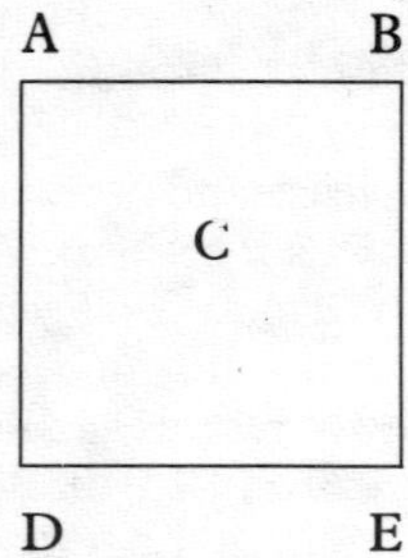

By A write the alcohol content of the spirit to be used for fortification, say 40 per cent.
By B the alcohol content of the wine to be fortified, say 16 per cent.
By C write the alcohol content required in the wine after it has been fortified, say 20 per cent.
By D write the difference between C and B, i.e. 20−16=4.
By E write the difference between A and B i.e. 40−20=20.

The ratio of D to E is the proportion of spirit required to fortify the wine as required, i.e. 4 to 20, or one bottle of spirit for every five bottles of wine. If Polish spirit was used only half a bottle would be needed.

Sweet table wines

These wines in the Sauternes/Barsac style, can be made from suitable ingredients, particularly peaches. Use sufficient sugar to produce about 12 per cent alcohol and leave enough residual sugar to sweeten the wine. A total sugar content of around 1.135 kg/2½ lb is indicated. It is important to use a Sauternes wine yeast since this leaves some residual fructose and creates more glycerine than other yeasts.

Ferment the must in the usual way, checking the specific gravity every few days. When the reading falls to about 1.016 siphon the wine from its sediment into a demijohn containing two crushed Campden tablets and a quarter teaspoonful of potassium sorbate. Seal the jar and move it to a cold place for about a week while the wine clears. Then filter the wine into bottles, seal them with good corks and store them in a cold place until the wine is mature.

The hydrometer

The importance of this instrument in the making of wine, beer, cider and mead cannot be over-emphasized. It measures the weight of a given volume of liquid against the same volume of water at a prescribed temperature. This figure is always printed on the hydrometer chart. If the temperature of the liquid to be tested is different from that prescribed on the hydrometer, then an allowance must be made. The prescribed figure on most hydrometers is 15°C/59°F. The last figure of the specific gravity reading must be increased if the liquid to be tested has a temperature higher than 15°C.

Temperature of liquid:

15°C/ 59°F no change
20°C/ 68°F no change
25°C/ 77°F add 2 to the final figure
30°C/ 86°F add 3.5 to the final figure
35°C/ 95°F add 5 to the final figure
40°C/104°F add 7 to the final figure

It follows then that the temperature of all liquids to be tested should first be checked and noted.

When testing a liquid it should be as clear as possible and if necessary, a sufficient quantity should be strained through a finely woven cloth. This will remove any particles of pulp which would distort the figures. Even so, the liquid may well contain some dissolved acids, mineral salts, tannins and vitamins, as well as the sugars that we particularly want to measure. If appropriate, especially at the beginning of a fermentation, an allowance should be made for these items by reducing the total reading by up to four points depending on the liquid itself. The weight of the sugar present can then be fairly closely, although not precisely, calculated by reference to the following chart.

specific gravity 15°C/59°F	*sugar in* 4.54 litres/1 gallon grams	ounces	*probable % alcohol after fermentation to dryness*
1.006	90	3.2	0.4
1.010	138	4.9	1.0
1.014	183	6.5	1.6
1.020	252	9.0	2.4
1.026	320	11.5	3.2
1.030	371	13.2	3.7
1.034	418	14.9	4.3
1.040	494	17.5	5.1
1.046	555	19.8	5.9
1.050	603	21.4	6.5
1.056	678	24.1	7.3
1.060	726	25.8	7.9
1.064	766	27.3	8.5
1.070	841	30.0	9.3
1.076	910	32.4	10.1
1.080	963	34.2	10.6
1.086	1136	36.9	11.4
1.090	1081	38.5	12.0
1.094	1134	40.4	12.6
1.100	1198	42.7	13.4
1.104	1241	44.2	14.0
1.110	1319	47.0	14.9
1.116	1386	49.4	15.7
1.120	1436	51.2	16.3
1.126	1510	53.8	17.2
1.130	1556	55.5	17.8

Other factors can affect the hydrometer readings. When testing a fermenting liquid the bubbles of carbon dioxide cling to the instrument and give it a buoyancy that lifts it up and, therefore, gives a false reading. Accordingly, a sample of such a liquid should be stirred vigorously to dissipate the carbon dioxide and then tested.

Towards the end of fermentation, after 10 per cent or more of alcohol may have been formed, the alcohol which is thinner and lighter than water, will have diluted the liquid to some extent. Thus a reading, after fermentation, of 1.000 does not mean that all the sugar has been converted. On the contrary, it means that some sugar still remains and that the alcohol has diluted the water. A really dry wine with minimal residual sugar will have a specific gravity of 0.990 or 0.992.

When using the hydrometer to calculate the alcohol content of a liquid, the original specific gravity must form the starting point, i.e. the specific gravity of the liquid prior to the admission of the yeast. The final specific gravity is then deducted thus calculating the total number of points fermented.

If a must is being fermented-on with added doses of sugar, the specific gravity readings should be noted before and after the sugar has been mixed in. The various number of units fermented should be recorded and finally added together to give a more accurate guide.

Adding sugar to a must increases its volume. Half the weight of the sugar added is the equivalent of the fluid measure. For example, the addition of 100g/4oz sugar increases the volume by 56ml/2floz. This marginally reduces the percentage of alcohol in the increased volume, but by so small a figure as to be insignificant.

Many hydrometers provide an alcohol percentage beside the specific gravity reading. This indicates the approximate percentage of alcohol that will be formed if all sugar in that liquid is fermented out. It does not mean that the liquid already contains that quantity of alcohol.

All these provisos enhance the accuracy of the hydrometer that we use in the home. By using it properly and regularly better table wines can be produced. All too often the sugar present in a base ingredient is overlooked and too much additional sugar is mixed in, causing too much alcohol to be produced and the balance of the wine to be changed.

Although the hydrometer or saccharometer as it was first called, has been available since around 1800, there are still far too many home wine-makers and brewers who do not trouble to use it, or who use it wrongly. Always check the specific gravity of a must or wort before adding any more sugar and only add sufficient to produce the approximate amount of alcohol you require. Always check the specific gravity of wines and beers when fermentation has stopped, and be sure not to seal the jars or bottles if any fermentable sugar remains in them. Wise use of the hydrometer can prevent burst bottles and jars and all the mess they cause. It can also prevent many a sore head by enabling the approximate quantity of alcohol produced to be carefully controlled.

Wine recipes

Each recipe has been set out with a fair amount of detail to save frequent cross references, but these general notes will also be found helpful.

Quantities These have been given in both metric and imperial measures. Some ingredients, for example sugar, are now only marketed in metric quantities. Others, such as fresh fruit, are still sold in imperial quantities. In general, the British have still not mastered metric volumes or temperatures, and continue to think in terms of pints and degrees Fahrenheit. Accordingly, the measures given have been fairly closely equated and it doesn't matter whether you use some metric and some imperial in the same recipe. Each one is designed on the unit of six standard bottles of wine. You can increase this quantity as you will as long as you increase each ingredient, except yeast, *pro rata*. A sachet of dried yeast granules or a compressed yeast tablet, or a phial of liquid yeast, is enough to ferment from one to six gallons.

Some containers of fruit juice or fruits, may contain a little more or a little less than that given in the recipe. For example, some cans of fruit contain 440 g/15½ oz and others may contain 454 g/1 lb; or some containers of fruit juice may contain 1 litre/35 fl oz, while others contain 1.1 litre/39 fl oz. These differences are of no consequence to the finished wine. Use all the contents of the container and if necessary adjust the amount of water accordingly.

The quantity of water suggested can never be more than an

approximate figure. The precise quantity will depend on the quantity of juice that you can extract from fresh fruit, the size of the container of canned fruit or juice, the size of your fermentation vessel and so on. If you produce a little more must than the fill of your container, ferment the surplus in a bottle beside the demijohn and use it for topping up. Whenever possible, top up with wine of the same or a similar kind, but failing that use a small quantity of cold boiled water.

Sugar Granulated white sugar is recommended for all recipes with but few exceptions. The caramel or toffee-like flavour of brown sugar enhances the flavour of Madeira style wines, but ruins others.

Grape additive All recipes recommend the addition of some fresh grapes, grape juice, concentrated grape juice, sultanas or raisins. Long experience has shown the advantages of this. Naturally use fresh grapes, grape juice or concentrated grape juice of the same colour as the wine you wish to produce. As a rule of thumb, you need approximately four times as much fresh grape or grape juice as you do of concentrated grape juice or sultanas or raisins. But all of these sources of the same fruit are interchangeable and you can use the one most convenient to you.

Containers of concentrated grape juice vary. Most are in 1 kg/2¼ lb cans to make up into six bottles of wine. Some are in 560 ml/1 pint plastic bottles that produce the same quantity of wine. From both of these containers take about a quarter of the contents. If the container is then sealed with a polythene lid or a screw stopper, whichever the case may be, and stored in the refrigerator it will keep for several months without deteriorating.

Boots sell small containers of concentrated grape juice specifically for adding to a gallon of must. The cans vary in size very slightly from time to time, and may contain 250 g or 240 g. This, too, is of no significance, just use all the contents. Indeed, some experienced wine-makers use less than the quantity recommended in these recipes; some use only 170 g or even 125 g. At first you are strongly recommended to use the larger quantity of 240/250 g per gallon to ensure good results right from the start.

Acid Some fruits contain so much acid that no more is needed in the recipe. Where an acid is required, you do not have to use that recommended. Use the one most readily available to you, but don't omit it.

Pectic enzyme There are a number of different brands available and a recommended dose is given on the label. Usually it is one 5ml teaspoonful, but some brands require more. Use the quantity recommended on the label of the brand you are using.

Yeast Each recipe recommends the use of a particular strain of yeast because long experience has shown the benefit of so doing. You can, however, use a different strain if you wish or an all-purpose wine yeast may be used instead of those recommended. But *do not* use baker's or brewer's yeast in wine musts.

Yeasts are best bought in sealed sachets sufficient for one fermentation. Drums of yeast compound could deteriorate before you have emptied the drum unless you are making a very large number of different wines in a short space of time.

Nutrient Although some sachets of dried yeast granules also contain a few crystals of a nutrient salt and of granulated sugar, this is only sufficient for the activation of the yeast prior to mixing it into the must. When nutrient is mentioned in the recipes, use one compressed nutrient tablet or one level 5 ml spoonful of a nutrient salt such as diammonium phosphate or ammonium sulphate, or a mixture of both.

Fermentation on the pulp This period begins not when the activated yeast is added, but when fermentation actually begins and the pulp rises to the surface. Keep the container well covered, although not so closely that the fermentation gas cannot escape. Keep the pulp moist at all times, preferably by a weighted plate. The period of time mentioned in the recipe should not be exceeded by more than a day in case too many bitter substances are extracted that give a coarse flavour to the wine.

Alcohol The total quantity of sugar in the must forms the alcohol and any residual sweetness. Up to a point, more sugar means more alcohol. Sweet and dessert wines may be stronger but there is much merit in well balanced wines containing between 10.5 and 12.5 per cent of alcohol. These can be enjoyed with food or by themselves. Only experienced wine-makers able to control, fairly accurately, the total acids, nutrients and sugars in their must, as well as their fermentation with high quality yeasts at the right temperatures are likely to get 6 per cent of alcohol from 450 g/1 lb sugar. Most people will be lucky to get as much and are likely to get a little less, especially after topping up. Use this as a rule of thumb then, but do not pile in the sugar to make stronger wines, except for aperitif and dessert wines usually consumed in smaller quantities.

Fermentation temperature A figure is often given as the desirable temperature to ferment a must once it has got started. A longer, slower fermentation for white wines enhances their bouquet and flavour and avoids the coarseness sometimes caused by fermentation at a higher temperature. The precise temperature is not critical, however. Once you have grasped the concept, ferment at the temperature most convenient to you.

Storage A period of storage is given for each recipe, but this, too, is only a guide. Some wines mature much more quickly than others and, annoyingly, the same recipe will produce a wine that matures more quickly one year than another. It happens commercially, too. Drink your wine when you think that it tastes most pleasant. When first made, it is likely to taste harsh, especially red wine. Try to keep some bottles long enough to mature fully. To help you, a number of recipes are given for wines that do mature quickly, especially the fruit juice, canned fruits and jam wines. Whilst these are not *great* wines, they are extremely pleasant and enjoyable and will give you the courage to be patient while other wines develop more slowly.

Food Many of the recipes indicate the sort of food that the wine accompanies. This is meant only as a guide and you can, of course, drink the wine of your choice with the food of your choice. The temperature recommendations are more important, however, and you are strongly advised to take note of them.

Apple wine 1

assorted apples	5 kg/11 lb	pectic enzyme and Campden tablets
sultanas	250 g/9 oz	Champagne wine yeast and nutrient
white sugar	500 g/18 oz	no acid required

Pour 2 litres/3½ pints cold water into a bin, add the pectic enzyme and one crushed Campden tablet.

Wash the apples, remove and discard any bruised or damaged parts, then crush or cut up the good apples into thin pieces, including the skin and core, but do not include any cut pips. Drop the fruit into the water as soon as it is crushed or cut. Wash and chop the sultanas and add these to the bin. Cover and leave for 24 hours.

Next day activate the yeast and stir it into the must. Replace the cover, leave for one week, gently pressing down the floating fruit twice each day.

Strain out, press dry and discard the fruit, stir in the sugar and when it is completely dissolved, pour the must into a demijohn, fit an airlock and leave to ferment out in a temperature around 15°C/59°F.

Rack the clearing wine from its sediment, top up, add one Campden tablet, seal and store for six weeks.

Rack again and store for at least one year.

Serve this fine dry white wine cold as an aperitif or as an accompaniment to baked fish, chicken, pork or ham.

Notes: Frozen apples may be used instead of fresh apples.

It is important always to use as many eating apples as possible and not to use too many cooking apples because of their high acidity.

Apples with little flavour produce wine of little flavour. Always use a mixture of different varieties.

Flavour can be improved by the use of about 500 g/18 oz of the sweet smelling cydonia japonica, quince, or by the addition of about 30 cloves.

Several batches of apple wine made throughout the autumn should be blended together in the spring to produce a better balanced wine.

Larger batches of this recipe may be made by increasing all the quantities *pro rata* – except the yeast. One sachet or tablet of yeast is enough for up to 23 litres/5 gallons.

Apple wine 2

apple juice	2 litres/3½ pints
concentrated grape juice	250 g/9 oz
white sugar	500 g/18 oz
citric acid	5 ml/1 tsp

pectic enzyme and Campden tablets

Champagne wine yeast and nutrient

Mix together in a demijohn the apple juice, concentrated grape juice, pectic enzyme, 1.1 litres/2 pints of water and one crushed Campden tablet. Cover and leave for 24 hours.

Boil the sugar and citric acid in 560 ml/1 pint of water for 20 minutes, and leave it to cool. Activate the yeast.

Mix in the sugar syrup, the activated yeast and nutrient. Fit an airlock and leave the jar in a warm place.

As soon as fermentation in the jar is vigorous, top up with cold water and move the jar to a cool place, 15°C/59°F, and leave until fermentation is finished.

Rack into a storage jar, add one Campden tablet and store for six months before bottling. Serve this wine cold as for Apple Wine 1.

Note: Cartoned apple juice from a supermarket is recommended. Instead of the concentrated grape juice, a carton of fresh grape juice may be used. Reduce the quantity of water used accordingly.

Apricot wine 1

fresh apricots	1.8 kg/4 lb	pectic enzyme and Campden tablets
sultanas	250 g/9 oz	Chablis wine yeast and nutrient
white sugar	680 g/1½ lb	no acid required

Pour the water into a bin, add the pectic enzyme and one crushed Campden tablet.

Stalk, wash and stone the apricots, then crush or cut up the fruit and add to the bin. Discard all the stones and stalks. Wash and chop the sultanas and add these to the bin. Cover the bin and leave for 24 hours.

Activate the yeast and mix this into the must, together with a nutrient tablet or one level teaspoonful of diammonium phosphate. Replace the cover and leave for four days, but gently press down the floating fruit cap twice daily.

Strain out, press dry and discard the pulp, stir in the sugar, pour the must into a demijohn, fit an airlock and ferment to a finish in a temperature around 15°C/59°F.

Rack into a storage jar, top up, add one Campden tablet, seal and store until the wine is bright, then rack again.

Mature this wine in bulk for one year before bottling, then keep for a further six months. Serve it cold with all fish dishes.

Apricot wine 2

dried apricots	340 g/12 oz	nutrient	5 ml/1 tsp
sultanas	250 g/9 oz	pectic enzyme and Campden tablets	
white sugar	680 g/1½ lb		
citric acid	5 ml/1 tsp	all-purpose wine yeast	

Wash the apricots and sultanas, chop them up, place them in a bowl, cover them with boiling water and leave overnight for the fruit to reconstitute.

Empty the fruit and any liquor into a bin, add 3.36 litres/6 pints of cold water, mix in the pectic enzyme, half the acid and one crushed Campden tablet. Cover and leave for 24 hours.

Activate the yeast and mix it into the pulp, replace the cover and ferment for three days, keeping the fruit submerged or gently pressed down twice each day.

Boil the sugar and the rest of the acid in the pint of water for 20 minutes, then leave it to cool.

Strain out, press dry and discard the pulp, mix in the sugar syrup, pour the must into a demijohn, top up, fit an airlock and ferment out.

Rack into a storage jar, top up, add one Campden tablet, seal and store in a cold place for four weeks, then rack again.

Mature this well-flavoured wine for one year in bulk and at least three months in the bottle.

If needs be, slightly sweeten it with saccharin (one tablet per bottle). Serve it cold.

Apricot wine 3 (makes 12 bottles)

canned apricot pieces	1.5 kg/3½ lb	pectic enzyme and Campden tablets
grape juice	1 litre/1¾ pints	Hock yeast and nutrient
white sugar	1.5 kg/3½ lb	wine stabilizer
citric acid	10 g/2 tsp	

Open the can of apricot pieces, strain off and save the syrup, empty the fruit into a polythene bin and crush it with a potato masher. Pour on 5.5 litres/10 pints of water and mix in the grape juice, pectic enzyme, half the acid and two crushed Campden tablets. Cover and leave for 24 hours.

Activate the yeast and stir this into the must together with one level teaspoonful of nutrient and the apricot syrup. Cover the bin and ferment on the pulp for three days, keeping the floating fruit submerged with a china plate.

Strain out the pulp through a large nylon sieve, shake it to extract as much juice as possible but do not squeeze it in case too much fine pulp is carried over.

Boil the sugar with the rest of the acid in 1.1 litres/2 pints of water for 20 minutes, leave to cool, then mix it into the must.

Pour equal quantities into two demijohns, top up if necessary, fit airlocks and ferment out in a temperature of around 15°C/59°F.

Check the specific gravity from time to time and as soon as the reading falls to 1.010 rack the wine into storage jars each containing a wine stabilizing tablet, or a quarter teaspoonful of potassium sorbate and once crushed Campden tablet.

Seal the jars and leave them in a cool place until the wine is bright. Bottle at once and keep this light, slightly sweet wine for another month or two.

Serve it chilled in warm weather.

Apricot wine 4

apricot jam	1.35 kg/3 lb	citric acid	5 g/1 tsp
concentrated grape juice	230 g/8 oz	pectic enzyme	double dose
white sugar	100 g/3½ oz	Campden tablets	
		Hock wine yeast and nutrient	

Use only jam that is free from additional pectin and preservative. Dissolve it in warm water and, when cool, mix in the contents of a small can of concentrated grape juice, the double dose of pectic enzyme, the acid, and one crushed Campden tablet. Cover and leave for 24 hours.

Strain out any solid particles, stir in the sugar, nutrient and an activated yeast, pour the must into a demijohn, top up, fit an airlock and ferment out.

Rack into a storage jar, top up, add one Campden tablet, seal and keep until the wine is bright. Siphon into bottles, adding one saccharin pellet to each, cork and keep for four months.

Serve this fast maturing wine nicely chilled.

Apricot wine 5

apricot 'Nectar'	600 ml/1 pint	pectic enzyme and Campden tablets
grape juice	600 ml/1 pint	Hock yeast and nutrient
white sugar	800 g/1¾ lb	
citric acid	5 g/1 tsp	

Empty the apricot and grape juices into a demijohn containing 2.2 litres/4 pints of cold water, the pectic enzyme and one crushed Campden tablet. Seal and leave in a warm place for 24 hours.

Boil the sugar and acid in one pint of water, and leave to cool. Activate the yeast.

Mix in the sugar syrup, nutrient and yeast, fit an airlock and ferment out.

Rack into a storage jar, top up, add one Campden tablet, seal and store until the wine is bright.

Siphon into bottles, add one saccharin pellet to each, cork and store for four months.

This is another fast maturing wine that should be served cold.

Banana wine

peeled bananas	1.8 kg/4 lb	pectic enzyme and Campden tablets
sultanas	250 g/9 oz	Sauternes wine yeast and nutrient
white sugar	680 g/1½ lb	wine stabilizer
citric acid	20 g/4 tsp	

Use very ripe bananas the skins of which have turned brown. Green bananas are not suitable. Peel the ripe bananas, discard the skins and mash the soft fruit with a fork. Place it in a bin with 4 litres/7 pints water, the washed and chopped sultanas, the citric acid, pectic enzyme and one crushed Campden tablet. Cover and leave for 24 hours.

Activate the yeast and add this with the nutrient to the must. Replace the cover and ferment on the pulp for four days, keeping the fruit submerged or gently pressed down twice each day.

Strain out and lightly press the pulp, stir in the sugar, pour the must into a demijohn, top up, fit an airlock and ferment down to SG 1.010 or just above.

Rack into a storage jar containing a crushed wine stabilizing tablet or a quarter teaspoonful of potassium sorbate, and one crushed Campden tablet. Top up, seal and store until the wine is bright, then rack again.

Mature this wine for one year in bulk and six months in bottle. Serve it chilled with sweet biscuits.

Beetroot wine

beetroot	2 kg/4½ lb	citric acid	15 g/3 tsp
concentrated grape juice	250 g/9 oz	grape tannin	5 g/1 tsp
brown sugar	1.15 kg/2½ lb	Sauternes wine yeast and nutrient	

Use fresh mature beetroot early in the autumn. Scrub them clean removing every trace of earth. Cut off the leaf stems and root and discard them. Slice the beetroots into thin pieces, place them in a large pan and boil them in 3.4 litres/6 pints water until they are soft but not mushy.

Strain the liquor into a polythene bin and leave it to cool. (The beetroot may be eaten as a vegetable and served with a white sauce; made into soup; or mixed with sliced onions and vinegar and served with salads.)

Stir in the concentrated grape juice, the citric acid, grape tannin, half the sugar and an activated wine yeast with nutrient. Pour the must into a demijohn, fit an airlock and leave in a warm place, 21–4°C/70–75°F.

After ten days, remove some must, stir in the remaining sugar and return this to the jar. Top up with cold water. Replace the airlock and leave until fermentation is finished.

Rack the wine into a dark storage jar, top up, seal and keep in a dark place for two years, then bottle and keep for a further three months. Serve it at room temperature with a sweet biscuit.

Note: The splendid red robe of this wine tends to fade when exposed to the light.

Bilberry wine 1

bottled bilberries	900 g/2 lb	grape tannin	5 g/1 tsp
concentrated grape juice	250 g/9 oz	pectic enzyme and Campden tablets	
sugar	900 g/2 lb	Bordeaux wine yeast and nutrient	
tartaric acid	5 g/1 tsp		

Empty the bilberries and syrup into a bin, crush the berries, add the concentrated red grape juice, 2.8 litres/5 pints of cold water, the pectic enzyme and one crushed Campden tablet. Cover and leave for 24 hours.

Add the activated wine yeast, nutrient and tannin, then ferment on the pulp for four days, keeping the fruit submerged and the bin covered.

Boil the sugar and acid in 560 ml/1 pint of water for 20 minutes and leave to cool.

Strain out, press dry and discard the bilberries, mix in the sugar syrup, pour the must into a demijohn, top up, fit an airlock and ferment out in a temperature of 21°C/70°F.

Rack into a storage jar, add one Campden tablet, seal and store until the wine is bright, then rack again. Keep for six months, then bottle and keep for a further three months.

Serve this well-flavoured dry table wine, free from chill, with red meat or cheese.

Note: It is better to use the concentrated red grape juice than sultanas since the grape juice improves the colour.

Bilberry wine 2

ripe bilberries*	1.5 kg/3¼ lb	grape tannin	5 g/1 tsp
ripe bananas	2	pectic enzyme and Campden tablet	
raisins	500 g/18 oz	Port wine yeast and nutrient	
sugar	1.25 kg/2¾ lb		

*Bilberries are sometimes called blueberries or whortleberries.

Pick the berries from their stalks, wash and crush them, add the peeled and mashed bananas and the washed and chopped raisins, place them in a bin and pour five pints of boiling water over them, cover and leave to cool.

Mix in the pectic enzyme and one crushed Campden tablet, cover and leave for 24 hours.

Activate the yeast and stir it into the must, together with the nutrient and tannin. Ferment on the pulp for four days, keeping the fruit submerged.

Dissolve the sugar in one pint of hot water and leave to cool.

Strain out, press dry and discard the fruit, mix in half the sugar, fit an airlock and ferment in a warm place for one week.

Add the rest of the syrup, top up with cold boiled water and ferment to a finish.

Rack into a storage jar, seal and store until the wine is bright, then rack again. Keep in bulk for at least one year and in bottle for as long as you can!

Serve this delicious, strong, sweet wine after the evening meal.

Bilberry wine 3

dried bilberries	340 g/12 oz	grape tannin	5 g/1 tsp
concentrated grape juice	250 g/9 oz	pectic enzyme and Campden tablets	
sugar	900 g/2 lb	Bordeaux wine yeast and nutrient	
tartaric acid	5 g/1 tsp		

Wash the bilberries in a sulphite solution, place them in a bin and pour 3 litres/5½ pints of boiling water over them, cover and leave to cool.

Add the pectic enzyme and one crushed Campden tablet, cover and leave for 24 hours.

Mix in the concentrated red grape juice, the activated yeast, the nutrient and tannin. Ferment on the pulp for four days, keeping the fruit submerged.

Boil the sugar and acid in one pint of water for 20 minutes and leave to cool.

Strain out, press dry and discard the bilberries, mix in the sugar syrup, pour the must into a demijohn, top up, fit an airlock and ferment out.

Rack into a storage jar, seal and keep for one year, then bottle.

Serve this dry red table wine with red meat or cheese.

Birch sap wine

birch sap	3.4 litres/6 pints	citric acid	15 g/3 tsp
concentrated white grape juice	250 g/9 oz	grape tannin	2.5 g/½ tsp
sugar	800 g/1¾ lb	all-purpose wine yeast and nutrient	

Simmer the birch sap in a covered pan for 10 minutes to sterilize it. Leave it to cool, then mix in the concentrated grape juice, two teaspoonsful of acid, the tannin and the activated yeast and nutrient.

Pour the must into a demijohn, fit an airlock and ferment at 16°C/61°F.

Boil the sugar and one teaspoonful of acid in 425 ml/¾ pint of water for 20 minutes and leave to cool. Mix this into the must as soon as it is fermenting vigorously, top up if necessary, then leave it to ferment out.

Rack into a storage jar, top up, add one Campden tablet, seal and store until the wine is bright, then rack again.

Keep for one year, then bottle and sweeten to taste with saccharin. Serve this wine cold.

Note: Sap should only be taken from mature trees early in March when the new sap is rising. You may kill the tree if you take the sap at a later date, or from an immature tree.

Bore a hole 1 cm/½ inch in diameter 35 cm/14 inches from the ground to a depth just below the bark – about 2 cm/1 inch. Push one end of a plastic tube into the hole, making a tight fit, and the other end into a sterilized demijohn placed on the ground at the foot of the tree. Plug the neck of the demijohn with cotton wool to keep out insects, and cover the jar with a sack to keep out the light. Leave for two to three days until about six pints of juice have been extracted.

Remove the tube and plug the hole in the tree with a piece of well fitting cork pushed in to the limit.

Blackberry wine 1

cultivated blackberries	2 kg/4½ lb	grape tannin	2.5 g/½ tsp
sultanas	250 g/9 oz	pectic enzyme and Campden tablets	
white sugar	680 g/1½ lb	Bordeaux wine yeast and nutrient	
citric acid	2.5 g/½ tsp		

Stalk, wash and crush the blackberries, wash and chop the sultanas, pour 2.8 litres/5 pints of boiling water over them, cover and leave to cool. Mix in the pectic enzyme and one crushed Campden tablet, replace the cover and leave for 24 hours.

Activate the yeast and mix it into the must together with the nutrient and tannin. Ferment on the pulp for four days, gently pressing the floating fruit cap down twice each day.

Boil the sugar and acid with 560 ml/1 pint of water for 20 minutes, then leave to cool.

Strain out, press dry and discard the pulp, mix in the sugar syrup, pour the must into a demijohn, top up, fit an airlock and leave in a temperature of 21°C/70°F until fermentation is finished.

Rack into a brown storage jar, top up, add one Campden tablet, seal and store until the wine is bright, then rack again. Keep this wine in a dark place to avoid fading for two years, then bottle and keep for a further six months.

Serve this dry red wine with roasted red meats, casseroles, pies, etc. If it is too dry for you, add one saccharin pellet per bottle.

Note: The bouquet and flavour may be enhanced by the addition of 200 g/7 oz of stalked, washed and crushed blackcurrants to the blackberries. Alternatives to blackcurrants for this purpose include raspberries and loganberries.

Blackberry wine 2

hedgerow blackberries	3 kg/6½ lb	citric acid	2.5 g/½ tsp
raisins	250 g/9 oz	grape tannin	2.5 g/½ tsp
white sugar	1 kg/2¼ lb	pectic enzyme and Campden tablet	
light brown sugar	340 g/¾ lb	Port wine yeast and nutrient	

Stalk, wash and crush the blackberries, wash and chop the raisins, pour 2.2 litres/4 pints of boiling water over them, cover and leave to cool.

Mix in the pectic enzyme and one crushed Campden tablet, cover and leave for 24 hours.

Add the activated yeast, nutrient and tannin, and ferment on the pulp for five days, keeping the pulp submerged.

Boil the two sugars and the acid in 560 ml/1 pint of water for 20 minutes, then leave to cool.

Strain out, press dry and discard the fruit, stir in half the syrup, pour the must into a demijohn, fit an airlock and leave in a warm place for one week.

Remove the airlock, pour in half the remaining sugar, replace the airlock and continue fermentation.

One week later, repeat this process with the rest of the syrup, top up if necessary, leave the must to finish fermenting.

When the wine begins to clear, rack into a brown storage jar, top up, seal and keep in a cool, dark place until the wine is clear. Rack again and continue to store in the dark for a further two years. Bottle and keep this sweet red dessert wine for a further year, then serve after meals.

Note: Bouquet and flavour are improved by the addition of 200 g/7 oz of blackcurrants, raspberries or loganberries.

Blackberry wine 3

bramble jelly	1.35 kg/3 lb	pectic enzyme (double dose) and Campden tablets
concentrated grape juice	240 g/8 oz	Bordeaux wine yeast and nutrient
white sugar	100 g/3½ oz	
citric acid	5 g/1 tsp	

Use only jam that is free from additional pectin and preservative. Dissolve it in 3.7 litres/6½ pints warm water and when cool mix in the contents of a small can of concentrated grape juice, the double dose of pectic enzyme, the acid and one crushed Campden tablet. Cover and leave for 24 hours.

Stir in the sugar, nutrient and an activated yeast, pour the must into a demijohn, top up, fit an airlock and ferment to a finish.

Rack into a storage jar, top up, add one Campden tablet, seal, keep until the wine is bright. Siphon into bottles, adding one saccharin tablet to each if required, and keep for four months.

Serve this fast maturing wine free from chill as a dry red table wine.

Note: The flavour can be improved by replacing one jar of bramble jelly with one jar of blackcurrant jam.

Blackcurrant wine

blackcurrants	1 kg/2¼ lb	pectic enzyme and Campden tablet
dried currants	500 g/18 oz	Port wine yeast and nutrient
white sugar	1 kg/2¼ lb	no acid required

Stalk, wash and crush the blackcurrants, wash and crush the dried currants, pour 3 litres/5¼ pints hot water over them, cover and leave to cool.

Mix in the pectic enzyme and one crushed Campden tablet and leave for a further 24 hours.

Activate the yeast and mix it into the must with the nutrient and ferment on the pulp for five days, keeping the fruit submerged.

Dissolve the sugar in 700 ml/1¼ pints hot water and leave to cool.

Strain out, press dry and discard the fruit, mix in the sugar syrup, pour the must into a demijohn, fit an airlock and ferment to a finish in a warm place (21°C/70°F).

When the wine begins to clear, rack into a storage jar, top up, seal and store in a cool dark place until the wine is bright, then rack again. Keep for two years, then serve this strong sweet wine free from chill after the evening meal.

Note: Two very ripe bananas may be peeled, crushed and added to the blackcurrants to increase the body of the wine. One tablespoonful of BP glycerine may be added to the wine during storage to enhance the silky texture of the wine.

Blackcurrant 2

concentrated blackcurrant juice	340 ml/12 fl oz	white sugar	1 kg/2¼ lb
concentrated grape juice	250 g/9 oz	tartaric acid	5 g/1 tsp
		Bordeaux wine yeast and nutrient	

Dissolve the blackcurrant juice and grape juice in about 2.2 litres/4 pints of water and give it a good stir or shake up in a demijohn to dissipate the preservative in the blackcurrant juice.

Dissolve the sugar and acid in 560 ml/1 pint of hot water, bring to the boil then leave to cool.

Add half the syrup to the must, mix in an activated yeast and nutrient, fit an airlock and ferment for ten days in a warm place (21°C/70°F).

Mix in the rest of the syrup, top up, and ferment out.

Rack into a brown storage jar, top up, seal and store until the wine is bright, then bottle and keep for three months.

Serve this wine dry with cheese and biscuits, or sweeten it to your taste.

Note: *Redcurrant syrup* is occasionally imported from Eastern Europe. It may be used in the manner described above, to make a rosé wine. The added sugar should be reduced by 200 g/7 oz and the wine finished with a hint of sweetness, i.e. one, or at the most two, saccharin pellets per bottle.

Bramble folly

Young blackberry shoots	3 kg/6½ lb	Campden tablets	
blackcurrant leaves	125 g/4½ oz	citric acid	15 g/3 tsp
grape juice	1 litre/1¾ pints	grape tannin	2.5 g/½ tsp
white sugar	800 g/1¾ lb	Hock wine yeast and nutrient	

Wash and cut up into small pieces the tender shoots and leaves, then boil them gently in 2.2 litres/4 pints of water for half an hour in a covered preserving pan. Strain out and discard the solids and when the liquor is cool, mix in the carton of grape juice or a 240 g/8 oz can of concentrated white grape juice. Add two teaspoonsful of acid, the tannin and an activated yeast. Then pour the must into a demijohn. Fit an airlock and leave in a warm place for 24 hours.

Boil the sugar and one teaspoonful of acid in one pint of water for 20 minutes and when it is cool, mix it into the must. Top up the jar with cold water and move it to a cooler place 16°C/61°F.

When fermentation is finished and the wine begins to clear, rack it into a storage jar, top up, add one crushed Campden tablet, seal and store until the wine is bright. Rack again and keep for six months.

Serve this wine cold with vegetarian meals. Sweeten it slightly with saccharin if necessary.

Broad bean wine

broad beans (shelled)	2 kg/4½ lb	citric acid	15 g/3 tsp
concentrated grape juice	250 g/9 oz	grape tannin	2.5 g/½ tsp
white sugar	680 g/1½ lb	Hock wine yeast and nutrient	
		Campden tablet	

Use old broad beans at the end of the season. Shell them and discard the husks.

Boil them in 3.4 litres/6 pints of water until they are soft but not mushy. Strain out the beans and serve them as a vegetable with or without a white sauce.

Dissolve the sugar and acid in the liquor, cover and leave to cool.

Mix in the concentrated grape juice, an activated yeast, nutrient and tannin. Pour the must into a demijohn, top up, fit an airlock and ferment out.

Rack into a storage jar, top up, add one Campden tablet, seal and store until the wine is bright, then rack again. Keep this wine for one year, then serve it cold as a light dry white table wine.

Note: A variation on this recipe: Replace 1 litre/1¾ pints of the water with 1 litre of apple juice from a supermarket and reduce the sugar by 110 g/4 oz.

Bullace wine

bullaces	2 kg/4½ lb	pectic enzyme and Campden tablet
sultanas	250 g/9 oz	Bordeaux wine yeast and nutrient
white sugar	900 g/2 lb	no acid required
grape tannin	5 g/1 tsp	

Stalk, wash, stone and crush the bullaces, which should be blue/black and fully ripe. Wash and chop the sultanas, add to the bullaces and pour hot water over them. Cover and leave to cool.

Add the pectic enzyme and one crushed Campden tablet, cover and leave in a warm place for 24 hours. Mix in the activated yeast, nutrient and tannin, and ferment on the pulp for four days, keeping the fruit gently pressed down twice each day.

Strain out, press dry and discard the pulp, stir in the sugar, pour the must into a demijohn, fit an airlock and ferment to a finish.

Rack into a storage jar, top up, add one Campden tablet and store in a cool, dark place until the wine is bright. Rack again and keep for one year before bottling.

Serve this wine free from chill with red meats.

Carrot wine

carrots	2 kg/4½ lb	grape tannin	5 g/1 tsp
concentrated grape juice	250 g/9 oz	pectic enzyme and Campden tablets	
sugar	1 kg/2¼ lb	Sauternes wine yeast and nutrient	
citric acid	15 g/3 tsp		

Scrub every trace of soil from the carrots, remove the crown and root, then cut them into thin slices. Place these in a pan, add 2.8 litres/5 pints of water and boil them until they are soft but not mushy.

Strain out the carrots and serve them as a vegetable. Cover the liquor and leave to cool.

Mix in the concentratred grape juice, two teaspoonsful of citric acid, the pectic enzyme and one crushed Campden tablet. Pour the must into a demijohn, seal and leave for 24 hours.

Activate the yeast and add this with the nutrient and tannin to the must. Fit an airlock and leave in a warm place (21°C/70°F).

Boil the sugar and one teaspoonful of acid in 560 ml/1 pint of water for 20 minutes and leave to cool.

As soon as fermentation is vigorous, add the sugar syrup to the must in two equal doses, one week apart.

When fermentation is finished, rack into a storage jar and keep until bright, then rack again and keep for two years in bulk. Siphon into bottles, sweetening with saccharin to taste if necessary, and keep for a further three months.

Serve cold with sweet biscuits.

Cherry wine 1

mixed cherries	2 kg/4½ lb	pectic enzyme and Campden tablets	
sultanas	250 g/9 oz	Bordeaux wine yeast and nutrient	
sugar	600 g/21 oz		
citric acid	10 g/2 tsp		
grape tannin	2.5 g/½ tsp		

Stalk, wash and stone the cherries, add the washed and chopped sultanas, the acid, and pectic enzyme. Pour 3.7 litres/6½ pints of cold water over them, stir gently, cover and leave for 24 hours in a warm place.

Mix in the activated yeast, nutrient and tannin, and ferment on the pulp for four days, gently pressing down the floating fruit cap twice each day.

Strain out, press dry and discard the fruit, stir in the sugar, pour the must into a demijohn, top up, fit an airlock and ferment to dryness.

Rack into a storage jar, top up, add one Campden tablet, seal and store until the wine is bright, then rack again.

Keep for one year and serve chilled as a dry table wine.

Cherry wine 2

morello cherries	2 kg/4½ lb	tartaric acid	10 g/2 tsp
raisins	250 g/9 oz	grape tannin	2.5 g/½ tsp
ripe bananas	2	pectic enzyme and Campden tablets	
white sugar	750 g/28 oz		
brown sugar	250 g/9 oz	Port wine yeast and nutrient	

Stalk, wash and stone the cherries, wash and chop the raisins, peel and mash the bananas, and drop all the fruit into a bin containing 2.8 litres/5 pints of cold water in which the pectic enzyme, one teaspoonful of tartaric acid and one Campden tablet have been dissolved. Cover and leave for 24 hours.

Mix in the activated yeast, nutrient and tannin, and ferment on the pulp for five days, keeping the fruit cap submerged.

Boil the sugar and one teaspoonful of acid in 850 ml/1½ pints of water for 20 minutes, leave to cool then store this in a bottle until required.

Strain out, press dry and discard the pulp, mix in half the sugar syrup, pour the must into a demijohn, fit an airlock and leave in a warm place for ten days. Remove the airlock, pour in half the remaining syrup, replace the lock and continue the fermentation for another seven days.

Repeat the process with the last of the syrup, top up with cold water, then leave the must to finish fermenting.

Rack into a clean storage jar, top up, seal and store until the wine is bright, then rack again and store in a cool dark place for two years. Serve this strong sweet wine after the evening meal.

Cherry plum wine

cherry plums	2 kg/4½ lb	grape tannin	2.5 g/½ tsp
sultanas	250 g/9 oz	pectic enzyme and Campden tablets	
white sugar	750 g/1 lb 10 oz	Chablis wine yeast and nutrient	
citric acid	5 g/1 tsp		

Stalk, wash and stone the fruit, place it in a bin with the washed and chopped sultanas, the pectic enzyme and one crushed Campden tablet. Pour on 3.4 litres/6 pints of cold water and stir gently. Cover and leave for 24 hours.

Mix in the activated yeast, nutrient and tannin, cover and leave for four days, keeping the fruit submerged.

Boil the sugar and acid in 560 ml/1 pint of water for 20 minutes and leave to cool.

Strain out, press dry, and discard the pulp, mix in the sugar syrup, pour the must into a demijohn, top up, fit an airlock and ferment to dryness.

Rack into a storage jar, top up, add one Campden tablet, seal and store until the wine is bright, then rack again. Keep for one year in bulk, then bottle and keep for a further six months.

Serve chilled as a dry white table wine with fish, pork or poultry.

Crab-apple wine

crab-apples	4 kg/9 lb	Champagne wine yeast and nutrient	
sultanas	250 g/9 oz	no acid or tannin required	
white sugar	340 g/12 oz		
pectic enzyme and Campden tablets			

The John Downie crab-apple makes a good wine and the Siberian varieties have also been used successfully. The marble size crab-apples are too bitter and are not recommended.

Stalk, wash and crush the apples and drop them at once into a bin containing 2 litres/3½ pints water in which the pectic enzyme and one crushed Campden tablet have been dissolved. Cover and leave for 24 hours.

Mix in an activated yeast and ferment on the pulp for five days, keeping the pulp submerged.

Strain out, press dry and discard the pulp, stir in the sugar, pour the must into a demijohn, top up, fit an airlock and ferment to dryness.

Rack into a storage jar, top up, add one Campden tablet and keep in a cool place until the wine is bright, then rack again. Keep for one year then sweeten to taste with saccharin before serving chilled.

Damson wine

damsons	2 kg/4½ lb	pectic enzyme and Campden tablet
raisins	250 g/9 oz	
white sugar	1 kg/2¼ lb	Port wine yeast and nutrient
light brown sugar	250 g/9 oz	no acid required
grape tannin	5 g/1 tsp	

Stalk, wash and stone the damsons – a tedious but essential task – wash and chop the raisins. Place the fruit in a bin and pour on 2.8 litres/5 pints of hot water. Cover and leave to cool.

Stir in the pectic enzyme and one crushed Campden tablet, replace the cover and leave in a warm place for 24 hours.

Add the activated yeast, nutrient and tannin and ferment on the pulp for five days, keeping the fruit submerged.

Dissolve all the sugar in 850 ml/1½ pints of hot water and leave to cool.

Strain out, press dry and discard the pulp, stir in half the sugar syrup and pour the must into a demijohn. Fit an airlock and ferment for ten days in a warm place.

Remove the airlock, pour in half the remaining syrup, replace the airlock and continue fermentation for seven days.

Repeat this process with the remaining syrup, top up if necessary, and leave the must to finish fermenting.

Rack into a storage jar, top up, seal and store until the wine is bright, then rack again. Keep this strong, sweet wine in a cool dark place for two years or more.

Serve it free from chill after meals.

Dandelion wine

dandelion petals	1 litre/1¾ pints	sugar	250 g/9 oz
concentrated grape juice	1 kg/2¼ lb	Sauternes wine yeast	
		Campden tablet	

Pick the petals from their calyx and place them in a suitable container, pour on boiling water and rub the petals against the side of the container with the back of a plastic spoon to extract the fragrant essences. Cover and leave to cool but repeat this process several times.

Strain out, press dry and discard the petals, mix in the concentrated white grape juice and an activated wine yeast, pour the must into a demijohn, fit an airlock and leave in a temperature of around 18°C/64°F.

After ten days, remove some must, stir in the sugar, return this to the jar, top up, replace the airlock and ferment to a finish.

Rack into a storage jar, add one Campden tablet, seal and store until the wine is bright, then bottle, sweeten to taste with saccharin, seal and store until the wine is six months old.

Serve it cool as a social wine.

Date and lemon wine

dates	2 kg/2¼ lb	pectic enzyme and Campden tablets
lemons	5	
raisins	250 g/9 oz	Madeira wine yeast and nutrient.
brown sugar	680 g/1½ lb	

Chop up the dates and raisins and place them in a boiling pan, together with the very thinly pared rind of the lemons. Add 3.4 litres/6 pints of water and the strained juice of one lemon, then bring to the boil and simmer for 20 minutes.

Empty into a bin and leave to cool.

Mix in the pectic enzyme and strained juice of three more lemons, cover and leave for 24 hours.

Add the activated wine yeast and nutrient and ferment on the pulp for one week.

Boil the sugar and strained juice of the remaining lemon in one pint of water for 20 minutes, cool and bottle until required.

Strain out, press dry and discard the fruit, stir in half the syrup, pour the must into a demijohn, fit an airlock and ferment for one week in a warm place.

Add the remaining syrup, top up if necessary, and continue fermentation to the end.

Move the jar to a cool place for a few days to encourage the wine to clear, then rack into a storage jar, top up and seal. Store until bright, then rack again, add one crushed Campden tablet and store in a very warm place (50°C/122°F) for six months. Return to a cool store and keep for at least two years.

This wine has a slightly caramel flavour in the Madeira style.

Serve it cold as an aperitif.

Elderberry wine 1

elderberries	1 kg/2¼ lb	grape tannin	2.5 g/½ tsp
blackcurrants	250 g/9 oz	pectic enzyme and Campden tablets	
sultanas	250 g/9 oz		
white sugar	740 g/26 oz	Bordeaux wine yeast and nutrient	
citric acid	5 g/1 tsp		

Stalk, wash and crush the elderberries and blackcurrants; wash and chop the sultanas; place them all in a bin and pour on 3 litres/5½ pints of hot water, cover and leave to cool.

Mix in the pectic enzyme and one crushed Campden tablet, cover and leave for 24 hours.

Add the activated yeast, nutrient and tannin, and ferment on the pulp for four days, keeping the fruit submerged.

Boil the sugar and acid in 400 ml/¾ pint of water for 20 minutes, then leave to cool.

Strain out, press dry and discard the fruit, mix in the syrup, pour the must into a demijohn, top up, fit an airlock and ferment out in a warm place.

Rack into a storage jar, top up, add one Campden tablet, seal and store for at least one year.

Serve as a dry red table wine with red meats or cheese.

Note: The blackcurrants enhance the flavour of the elderberries. If fresh or frozen blackcurrants are not available, a jar of blackcurrant jam may be used instead, but increase the quantity of pectic enzyme used by half and decrease the quantity of sugar used by 230 g/8 oz.

Elderberry wine 2

elderberries	1 kg/2¼ lb	light brown sugar	250 g/9 oz
blackberries	1 kg/2¼ lb	citric acid	5 g/1 tsp
damsons	250 g/9 oz	grape tannin	2.5 g/½ tsp
bananas	2	pectic enzyme and Campden tablets	
raisins	250 g/9 oz	Port wine yeast and nutrient	
white sugar	1 kg/2¼ lb		

Stalk, wash and crush the elderberries and blackberries. Stalk, wash, stone and crush the damsons, peel and mash the bananas, wash and chop the raisins. Pour 2 litres/3¾ pints of hot water over them, cover and leave to cool.

Mix in the pectic enzyme and one crushed Campden tablet, cover and leave for 24 hours.

Stir in the activated wine yeast, nutrient and tannin, and ferment on the pulp for four days, keeping the pulp submerged.

Boil all the sugar and the acid in 800 ml/1⅓ pints of water for 20 minutes, then leave to cool.

Strain out, press dry and discard the pulp, stir in half the sugar syrup, pour the must into a demijohn, fit an airlock and leave in a warm place for ten days.

Mix in half the remaining syrup and one week later add the rest; top up, then leave the must to finish fermenting.

Rack into a storage jar, top up, seal and store until the wine is bright, then rack again.

Mature this strong, sweet dessert wine in a cool dark place for at least two years, then bottle and keep for as long as you can.

Note: If damsons are not available, sloes may be used instead. Other alternatives are blackcurrants, raspberries, loganberries or mulberries. These ingredients do much to enhance the finished flavour of the wine.

Elderberry wine 3

dried elderberries	250 g/9 oz	tartaric acid	10 g/2 tsp
concentrated grape juice	250 g/9 oz	pectic enzyme (double dose) and Campden tablets	
blackcurrant jam	450 g/1 lb	Bordeaux yeast and nutrient	
sugar	600 g/21 oz		

Wash the elderberries in a sulphite solution, place them in a bin and pour on 1.7 litres/3 pints of boiling water. Cover and leave to cool.

Dissolve the jam in 1.1 litres/2 pints of warm water, cover and leave to cool.

Mix together the elderberries and their liquor, the jam and its liquor, the concentrated red grape juice, the double dose of pectic enzyme, one teaspoonful of tartaric acid and one crushed Campden tablet. Cover and leave for 24 hours.

Mix in the activated yeast and nutrient, and ferment on the pulp for four days, keeping the fruit submerged.

Boil the sugar and one teaspoonful of acid in 560 ml/1 pint of water for 20 minutes, then leave to cool.

Strain out, press dry and discard the pulp, stir in the syrup, pour the must into a demijohn, fit an airlock and ferment out.

Rack into a storage jar, seal and store until the wine is bright then rack again.

Keep for one year in bulk, then bottle and store for another six months.

Serve this dry red table wine with red meats or cheese.

Elderberry punch

elderberry wine	1 bottle	cloves	12
lemon	1	honey	1 tablespoonful
dried ginger root	1 large piece	sugar to taste	

Pour the wine into a saucepan, then add the thinly pared rind of the lemon, the cloves and crushed dried ginger root.

Place on a low heat, then slowly stir in the honey until it is dissolved. Depending on the sweetness of the wine, add one or two tablespoonsful of sugar.

Stir slowly until it is dissolved.

Check the temperature of the punch and move it from the heat as soon as a reading of 60°C/140°F is recorded.

Cut the lemon in two, express all the juice and pour it into the saucepan. Taste the punch and if needs be stir in more sugar to suit your taste.

Replace the saucepan on to the stove and, as soon as the temperature of the punch again reaches 60°C/140°F, strain out the solids and pour the punch into pre-heated glasses. Serve at once with hot mince pies.

Elderflower wine

elderflower florets	560 ml/1 pint	sugar	250 g/9 oz
concentrated grape juice	1 kg/2¼ lb	Sauternes wine yeast	
		Campden tablet	

Pick the florets from their stalks and place them in a suitable container, pour on boiling water and rub the florets against the side of the container with the back of a plastic spoon to extract the fragrant essences. Cover and leave to cool but repeat this process several times.

Strain out, press dry and discard the florets, mix in the concentrated white grape juice and an activated wine yeast, pour the must into a demijohn, fit an airlock and leave in a temperature around 18°C/64°F.

After ten days, remove some must, stir in the sugar, return this to the jar, top up, replace the airlock and ferment to a finish.

Rack into a storage jar, add one Campden tablet, seal and store until the wine is bright, then bottle, sweeten to taste with saccharin, seal and store until the wine is six months old.

Serve it cool as a social wine.

Ginger wine

dried root ginger	85 g/3 oz	tartaric acid	15 g/3 tsp
cayenne pepper	2.5 g/½ tsp	all-purpose wine yeast and nutrient	
raisins	500 g/18 oz	green food colouring	
sugar	1.25 kg/2¾ lb		

Crush the well-broken dried root ginger and place it in a bin, together with the cayenne pepper, two teaspoonsful of acid and the chopped raisins. Pour on 2.8 litres/5 pints of boiling water, cover and leave to cool.

Add the activated yeast and nutrient and ferment for four days, keeping the fruit submerged.

Boil the sugar and remaining acid in 850 ml/1½ pints of boiling water and leave to cool.

Strain out, press dry and discard the pulp or mix into a chutney. Stir in the sugar syrup, pour the must into a demijohn, top up, fit an airlock and ferment to a finish.

Rack into a storage jar, seal and store until the wine is bright, then rack again. Add enough green food colouring to make the wine a rich green, and store for one year.

Serve this strong sweet wine after meals.

Gooseberry wine 1

gooseberries	1.35 kg/3 lb	pectic enzyme and Campden tablets
sultanas	250 g/9 oz	Hock wine yeast and nutrient
white sugar	750 g/26 oz	no acid required

For this recipe use the Careless variety of gooseberry if possible, but any cooking variety will do. Dessert gooseberries are not suitable. The gooseberries should be just fully ripe but not over-ripe.

Wash and crush the gooseberries. (If they are too hard to crush easily, cut them in two along their length with a sharp knife.)

Wash and chop the sultanas, pour on 3.4 litres/6 pints of cold water and mix in the pectic enzyme and one crushed Campden tablet. Cover and leave for 24 hours.

Add the activated yeast and nutrient, and ferment on the pulp for three days in a warm place, gently pressing down the fruit twice daily.

Dissolve the sugar in a pint of hot water and leave to cool.

Strain out, press dry and discard the pulp. Mix in the sugar syrup, pour the must into a demijohn, top up, fit an airlock and ferment out.

Rack into a storage jar, top up, add one Campden tablet, seal and store until the wine is bright, then rack again.

Keep this wine in a cool dark place for at least one year then serve it chilled as a light dry white wine. If it is too dry for your palate sweeten it slightly with saccharin at the rate of one or two tablets per bottle.

Gooseberry wine 2

gooseberries	1 kg/2¼ lb
grape juice	1 litre/1¾ pints
white sugar	750 g/26 oz
pectic enzyme and Campden tablets	
Champagne wine yeast and nutrient	

After six months:

white sugar	70 g/2½ oz
Champagne wine yeast	

Use similar gooseberries to the former recipe; wash and crush or cut them. Add the grape juice, 2.8 litres/5 pints water, pectic enzyme, and one crushed Campden tablet. Cover and leave for 24 hours.

Activate the yeast and nutrient and stir into the must. Ferment on the pulp for three days, keeping the floating fruit submerged.

Strain out, press dry and discard the pulp, stir in the sugar, pour the must into a demijohn, top up, fit an airlock and ferment to dryness in a cool temperature, around 16°C/61°F.

Rack into a storage jar, top up, add one Campden tablet, seal and store in a cold place until the wine is bright. Rack again and keep until the wine is six months old.

Remove a little of the wine, mix in precisely 70 g/2½ oz sugar, add the second Champagne wine yeast and return to the jar. Fit an airlock and leave the jar in a warm place.

Clean and prepare six 75 cl heavy Champagne bottles, six hollow-domed plastic stoppers and six wire cages.

As soon as the wine starts to ferment, siphon it into the prepared bottles leaving a 5 cm/2 in gap from the top of the bottle. Push the softened stoppers well home, wire on the cages, label the bottles with the date and lay them on their sides in a warm place for six days, and in a cool store for six months.

Grape wine 1

concentrated grape juice	1 kg/2¼ lb	wine yeast and nutrient
sugar approx	250 g/9 oz	Campden tablet

Mix the grape juice, sugar and 3.4 litres/6 pints water together and adjust the specific gravity with a little more water or sugar as may be necessary to achieve a specific gravity of 1.076 to 1.080 for white wines, and 1.086 to 1.090 for red wines.

Add the yeast, fit an airlock and ferment out. Rack into a storage jar, add one Campden tablet, seal and store until the wine is bright, then bottle and keep it until it is six months old.

Serve these dry wines with appropriate food.

They can be sweetened to taste with saccharin, if so desired.

Note: Some concentrates come in different-sized containers to make six bottles of wine. Adjust the water accordingly.

Grape wine 2

white grapes 8 kg/18 lb
pectic enzyme and Campden tablets
sugar to specific gravity between 1.076 and 1.080
Hock wine yeast

Stalk, wash and crush the grapes, add the pectic enzyme and one crushed Campden tablet, cover and leave for 24 hours.

Strain out, press dry and discard the skins, adjust the specific gravity, mix in an activated wine yeast, pour the must into a demijohn, fit an airlock and ferment out in a temperature of 16°C/61°F.

Rack into a storage jar, add one Campden tablet, seal and store until the wine is bright.

Siphon into bottles and keep for at least six months then serve cold as a dry white wine.

Grape wine 3

black grapes 8 kg/18 lb
pectic enzyme and Campden tablets
sugar to specific gravity 1.086 to 1.090
Burgundy wine yeast

Stalk, wash and crush the grapes, add the pectic enzyme and one crushed Campden tablet. Cover and leave for 24 hours.

Remove a sample of must, press the grapes, check the specific gravity of the juice, and add sugar as necessary.

Mix in an activated wine yeast and ferment on the pulp for ten days in a temperature of 20°C/68°F. Keep the fruit cap submerged or gently pressed down twice each day. It must not be allowed to dry out or attract fruit flies.

Strain out, press dry and discard the skins, pour the must into a demijohn, fit an airlock and ferment out.

Rack into a storage jar, fit a safety bung in case of a malo-lactic ferment and store for at least one year before bottling.

Serve free from chill with red meats or cheese.

Grape wine 4

black and white grapes 8 kg/18 lb
pectic enzyme and Campden tablets
sugar to specific gravity 1.080
Bordeaux wine yeast and nutrient

Stalk, wash and crush the grapes, add the pectic enzyme and one crushed Campden tablet, cover and leave for 24 hours.

Adjust the specific gravity, mix in the yeast and ferment for two or three days on the pulp until the must is a pretty pink.

Strain out, press dry and discard the skins, pour the must into a demijohn, fit an airlock and ferment out.

Rack into a storage jar, add one Campden tablet, seal and keep for six months, then bottle and keep for a further three months.

Serve this rosé wine cold with picnic sandwiches or party snacks.

Notes on the grape wines

Grapes grown in the UK may be rather high in acid and the wine made from them will, therefore, keep longer. Any excessive sharpness can be masked with one saccharin tablet per bottle.

Bought grapes, notably the small sultana grapes and dessert grapes, will be a little low in acid and will benefit from one level teaspoonful of tartaric acid.

The Italian wine grapes, when obtainable, make a splendid red wine that needs to be kept for at least two years.

Grapefruit wine

grapefruit juice 1 litre/35 fl oz
concentrated grape juice 250 g/9 oz
white sugar 1 kg/2¼ lb
pectic enzyme and Campden tablets
Burgundy wine yeast and nutrient

Pour 2 litres/3½ pints of water into a demijohn, add the grapefruit juice, concentrated grape juice, the pectic enzyme and one crushed Campden tablet. Seal and leave in a warm place for 24 hours.

Dissolve the sugar in the rest of the water, bring to the boil then leave to cool.

Activate the yeast and nutrient in a cupful of tepid water, then mix it into the must, together with half the syrup. Fit an airlock and ferment in a cool place, 17°C/63°F, for one week.

Pour in half the remaining syrup and four days later add the rest. Top up the jar with cold boiled water and ferment out.

Rack into a storage jar, add one Campden tablet and store for three months before bottling.

Serve cold as a dry aperitif.

Note: Some containers of grapefruit juice hold slightly more than 1 litre/1¾ pints. Any size from 1 to 1.25 litres is suitable. Reduce water accordingly.

Loganberry wine

loganberries	1 kg/2¼ lb	pectic enzyme and Campden tablets
raisins	250 g/9 oz	
sugar	1 kg/2¼ lb	Port wine yeast and nutrient
		no acid needed

Wash and crush the loganberries, wash and chop the raisins, place them in a bin and pour on 2.8 litres/5 pints hot water, cover and leave to cool.

Add the pectic enzyme and one crushed Campden tablet, cover and leave for 24 hours.

Activate the yeast in a cupful of tepid water and add this to the must.

Ferment on the pulp for four days, keeping the fruit submerged.

Dissolve the sugar in 560 ml/1 pint of hot water and, when cool, save it in a sealed bottle in the refrigerator.

Strain out, press dry and discard the pulp, stir in half the sugar syrup, pour the must into a demijohn, fit an airlock and ferment for seven days.

Mix in half the remaining syrup and, four days later, add the rest. Top up with cold boiled water and continue fermentation until it finishes.

Rack into a storage vessel, top up, seal and store for one year before bottling then keep for another year.

Sweeten the wine to taste before serving as a social wine.

Note: Loganberries contain a lot of acid and have a very strong flavour.

Mixed fruit wine 1

mixed fruit*	1.8 kg/4 lb	Bordeaux wine yeast and nutrient
sugar	1 kg/2¼ lb	stabilizing tablet
pectic enzyme and Campden tablets		

*Use small quantities (225 g/½ lb) of as many different summer fruits as you can. A few peeled bananas, some early blackberries, a few black, red and white currants, cherries, sultana grapes, loganberries, raspberries, strawberries, etc. Do include some grapes or at least some sultanas.

Clean, wash, stone, crush or liquidize the fruit, add the pectic enzyme, one crushed Campden tablet and 2.8 litres/5 pints water. Cover and leave for 24 hours.

Add an activated yeast and nutrient and ferment on the pulp for three days, keeping the fruit submerged or gently pressed down twice each day.

Dissolve the sugar in 560 ml/1 pint of hot water and leave to cool.

Strain out, press dry and discard the pulp, mix in the syrup, pour the must into a demijohn, top up, fit an airlock and ferment down to SG 1.004.

Rack into a storage jar containing a stabilizing tablet or 1 g/¼ tsp of potassium sorbate, and one crushed Campden tablet. Seal and store in a cold place until the wine is clear, then rack again and keep for one year.

Serve this well flavoured wine, nicely chilled, with picnic sandwiches or party snacks.

Mixed fruit wine 2

canned apricots	440 g/15½ oz	sugar	800 g/1¾ lb
canned gooseberries	440 g/15½ oz	tartaric acid	5 g/1 tsp
canned golden plums	440 g/15½ oz	pectic enzyme and Campden tablets	
concentrated white grape juice	250 g/9 oz	Hock wine yeast and nutrient	

Open the cans, drain off and save the light syrup, crush the fruit, removing and discarding the plum stones. Pour 2.8 litres/5 pints cold boiled water over the fruit and mix in the acid, pectic enzyme and one crushed Campden tablet, cover and leave for 24 hours.

Add the concentrated white grape juice, and an activated yeast and nutrient, then ferment on the pulp for three days, keeping the fruit submerged.

Strain out the pulp through a fine meshed nylon straining bag, roll the pulp around in the bag to extract as much juice as possible but do not press the pulp.

Stir in the sugar and the fruit syrup, pour the must into a demijohn, fit an airlock and ferment out.

Rack into a storage jar, top up, add one Campden tablet, seal and store until the wine is bright.

Siphon into bottles, add one saccharin pellet to each one, cork and keep until the wine is three to four months old.

Serve the wine nicely chilled on a hot day.

Note: Any combination of canned fruits may be used with equal success.

Mixed fruit wine 3

apple juice	1 litre/1¾ pints	sugar	1.5 kg/3¼ lb
grapefruit juice	1 litre/1¾ pints	tartaric acid	10 g/2 tsp
orange juice	1 litre/1¾ pints	pectic enzyme and Campden tablets	
pineapple juice	1 litre/1¾ pints	Hock wine yeast and nutrient	
concentrated grape juice	500 g/18 oz		

Mix together all the juices including the grape, add the pectic enzyme and one crushed Campden tablet. Cover and leave for 24 hours.

Boil the sugar, acid and 3.4 litres/6 pints water together for 20 minutes then leave to cool.

Mix an activated yeast and nutrient into the must and when fermentation has started, slowly stir in the sugar syrup.

Pour the must into two demijohns, fit airlocks and ferment out.

Rack into storage jars, add one Campden tablet to each, seal and store in a cool place.

As soon as the wine is bright, siphon into bottles and add one saccharin pellet to each bottle. Cork and keep until the wine is four months old, then serve it nicely chilled on a warm day.

Mulberry wine

purple ripe mulberries	1.5 kg/3½ lb	pectic enzyme and Campden tablets
sultanas	340 g/12 oz	Port wine yeast and nutrient
white sugar	1.25 kg/2¾ lb	no acid needed

Wash and crush the mulberries, wash and liquidize the sultanas, place them in a bin and pour 3.4 litres/6 pints boiling water over them. Cover and leave to cool.

Add the pectic enzyme and one crushed Campden tablet, cover and leave for 24 hours.

Mix in an activated wine yeast and nutrient, and ferment on the pulp for four days, keeping the pulp submerged.

Strain out, press dry and discard the pulp, stir in half the sugar, pour the must into a demijohn, fit an airlock and ferment for one week at 20°C/68°F.

Remove some must, gently stir in half the remaining sugar, return it to the jar and continue fermentation.

One week later repeat the process with the last of the sugar. Stir very gently so as not to dissipate the alcohol and developing esters.

Ferment to a finish then rack into a storage jar. Seal and store until the wine is bright, then rack again and store for two years in bulk and a further year in bottle. Sweeten to taste if desired just before serving as a post dinner dessert wine with walnuts or cheese.

Long storage is essential for this wine to develop its best bouquet and flavour.

Orange wine 1

Seville oranges (bitter)	6	sugar	1.35 kg/3 lb
navel oranges (sweet)	4	pectic enzyme and Campden tablets	
ripe bananas	5		
sultanas	250 g/9 oz	sherry wine yeast and nutrient	

Thinly pare three bitter oranges and two sweet ones, chop the parings and place them in a bin together with the peeled and mashed bananas and the washed and liquidized sultanas. Pour on approximately 2.2 litres/4 pints of boiling water, cover and leave to cool.

Express and strain out the juice from all the oranges and add to the bin together with some pectic enzyme and one crushed Campden tablet. Cover and leave for 24 hours.

Mix in an activated sherry yeast and ferment on the pulp for four days, keeping the fruit cap submerged.

Dissolve the sugar in a litre/1¾ pints of hot water and leave to cool, then bottle, seal and store it in the refrigerator.

Strain out, gently press then discard the pulp, mix in half the syrup, pour the must into a demijohn, fit an airlock and ferment at around 18°C/64°F for ten days.

Pour in half the remaining syrup and one week later add the rest. Top up the jar and ferment to a finish.

Rack into a storage jar, seal and store in a cold place until the wine is bright, then rack into two demijohns and plug the neck of each with cotton wool.

Store like this for at least one year and preferably longer. If you wish you can fortify the sherry flavour with one bottle of sherry of a similar style – dry or medium.

After two years bottle or blend with another sherry style wine. Serve this wine cold as an aperitif or sweeten it and serve as a social or dessert wine.

Orange wine 2

sweet oranges	10	pectic enzyme and Campden tablets
canned peaches	440 g/15½ oz	Sauternes wine yeast and nutrient
concentrated grape juice	250 g/9 oz	
sugar	800 g/1¾ lb	

Wash and thinly pare six oranges, chop them up and place them in a bin. Strain the syrup from the peaches and store it in the refrigerator.

Crush or liquidize the peaches, and add to the bin. Pour approximately 2.5 litres/4½ pints of boiling water over them, cover and leave to cool.

Express and strain the juice from all the oranges and add to the bin with the pectic enzyme and one crushed Campden tablet. Cover and leave for 24 hours.

Dissolve the sugar in a litre/1¾ pints of hot water, leave to cool then bottle, seal and store in the refrigerator.

Mix into the must the concentrated grape juice (sweet white wine style for preference) and the activated yeast and nutrient. Cover and ferment on the pulp for two days.

Strain out and lightly press the pulp, then discard it. Pour the must into a demijohn, add the peach syrup and the sugar syrup, top up, fit an airlock and ferment to a finish.

Rack into a storage jar, add two Campden tablets, seal and store until the wine is bright, then rack again.

Mature this wine for one year, then bottle and serve it cold with the dessert course of a meal as you would a Sauternes or Barsac.

If needs be sweeten it still further to your taste.

Orange wine 3

orange juice	1 litre/1¾ pints	pectic enzyme and Campden tablets
concentrated grape juice	250 g/9 oz	Burgundy wine yeast and nutrient
white sugar	1 kg/2¼ lb	
tartaric acid 5 g/1 tsp		

Boil the sugar and acid in 620 ml/21¾ fl oz water for twenty minutes, leave to cool, then store in a large bottle with a cork stopper.

Pour 2 litres/3½ pints of water into a demijohn, add the orange juice, concentrated grape juice, pectic enzyme and one Campden tablet. Seal and leave in a warm place for 24 hours.

Activate a sachet of wine yeast and nutrient in a cupful of water and mix it into the must, together with half the syrup, fit an airlock and ferment for a week in a cool place.

Mix in half the remaining syrup and one week later the rest. Top up with cold boiled water and ferment out.

Rack into a storage jar, top up, add one Campden tablet, seal and store until the wine is bright. Bottle and keep for three months, then serve cold as a dry aperitif, or sweeten it with saccharin to your taste.

Note: Some containers of juice hold more than 1 litre/1¾ pints. Any size from 1 to 1.25 litres is suitable. Reduce the water accordingly.

Orchard wine

assorted apples	2.7 kg/6 lb	pectic enzyme and Campden tablets
hard pears	900 g/2 lb	Champagne wine yeast and nutrient
quince	450 g/1 lb	no acid required
crab apples	450 g/1 lb	
sultanas	250 g/9 oz	
white sugar	500 g/18 oz	

Pour 2 litres/3½ pints cold water into a bin, add the pectic enzyme and one crushed Campden tablet.

Clean, wash and crush all the fruit, or cut it into thin slices. Drop it at once into the bin. Cover and leave for 24 hours.

Activate the yeast and add it with the nutrient to the bin. Replace the cover and leave for one week, gently pressing down the floating fruit twice each day.

Strain out, press dry and discard the pulp, stir in the sugar, pour the must into a demijohn, top up if necessary, fit an airlock and ferment to a finish in a temperature around 15°C/59°F.

Rack into a storage jar, top up, add one Campden tablet, seal and store for six weeks.

Rack again and keep for at least one year. Serve this fine dry white wine cold as an aperitif or with poultry, pork or ham.

Parsnip wine

fresh parsnips	2 kg/4½ lb	tartaric acid	15 g/3 tsp
concentrated grape juice	250 g/9 oz	Sauternes wine yeast and nutrient	
sugar	1.1 kg/2 lb 7 oz		

The parsnips should be well frosted and freshly dug. The best time to make this wine is about the end of January.

Remove the crowns and any rusty portions, scrub the parsnips free from every trace of earth, cut them into thin rings and boil them in 2.8 litres/5 pints of water until they are quite soft but not mushy.

Strain out and discard the parsnips and leave the liquor to cool.

Boil the sugar and one teaspoonful of the acid in 1 litre/1¾ pints water, leave to cool, then bottle, seal and store in the refrigerator.

Mix in the concentrated grape juice (sweet white wine style if possible), the acid, half the sugar syrup, and an activated yeast and nutrient.

Pour the must into a demijohn, fit an airlock and leave for ten days.

Mix in the remaining sugar syrup, top up and finish the fermentation.

When the wine begins to clear, rack into a storage jar, add one Campden tablet, top up, seal and store until the wine is bright, then rack again.

Keep this wine for at least one year, then sweeten it to taste, if necessary. Serve it cold as a social wine.

Parsnip and fig wine

fresh parsnips	2 kg/4½ lb	tartaric acid	15 g/3 tsp
sultanas	250 g/9 oz	sugar	1.35 kg/3 lb
dried figs	200 g/7 oz	sherry wine yeast and nutrient	

Prepare and boil the parsnips as previously described, then strain the hot liquor over the washed and chopped sultanas and figs. Cover and leave to cool.

Prepare the sugar syrup as also described above. Mix the rest of the acid, an activated yeast and the nutrient into the must and ferment the sultanas and figs on the pulp for four days, keeping the fruit cap submerged.

Strain out, press dry and discard the pulp, stir in half the sugar, pour the must into a demijohn, fit an airlock and ferment for ten days. Mix in half the remaining sugar and one week later add the rest, top up, then ferment to a finish.

Rack into a storage jar, seal and store until the wine is bright, then rack into a larger jar, leaving an airspace. Plug the neck of the jar with cotton wool and store for two years before bottling.

This is a medium sherry style wine; serve it cold at any time.

Passion fruit wine

passion fruit juice	560 ml/1 pint	pectic enzyme and Campden tablets
apple juice	1 litre/1¾ pints	Sauternes wine yeast and nutrient
grape juice	560 ml/1 pint	
sugar	650 g/1 lb 7 oz	
tartaric acid	5 g/1 tsp	

Mix the fruit juices together in a demijohn, add the pectic enzyme and one crushed Campden tablet, seal the jar and leave for 24 hours.

Boil the sugar, acid and 2 litres/3½ pints water together for 20 minutes and leave to cool.

Add half the sugar syrup, fit an airlock and ferment in a cool atmosphere (17°C/63°F) for four days, then add the rest of the syrup and ferment to a finish.

Rack into a storage jar, add one Campden tablet, seal and store until the wine is bright, then bottle and keep for six months.

Sweeten to taste, if necessary, then serve this wine cold at any time.

Peach wine 1

ripe peaches	1.5 kg/3½ lb	tartaric acid	10 g/2 tsp
concentrated grape juice	250 g/9 oz	pectic enzyme and Campden tablets	
sugar	900 g/2 lb	Sauternes wine yeast and nutrient	

Remove and discard the stones and skin, then liquidize or crush the fruit. Place it in a bin, pour on 2.3 litres/4 pints of cold water and mix in the pectic enzyme, half the acid and one crushed Campden tablet. Cover and leave for 48 hours.

Strain out the pulp through a fine meshed nylon straining bag, rolling the pulp around to extract as much juice as possible, but do not press it in case particles are carried forward into the must.

Mix in the concentrated grape juice (sweet white wine style for preference), together with an activated yeast and the nutrient.

Pour the must into a demijohn, fit an airlock and ferment at around 17°C/63°F for four days.

Boil the sugar and acid in 560 ml/1 pint of water, cover and leave to cool.

Mix all the syrup into the must, top up and ferment to a finish.

Rack the clearing wine into a demijohn, top up, add one Campden tablet, seal and store until the wine is bright. Rack again and store for nine months in bulk, then bottle and sweeten to taste with saccharin.

Serve this wine sweet and cold with the dessert course of a meal.

Note: The peaches should be fully ripe but not damaged. Any bruised parts should be cut out and discarded.

Peach wine 2

canned peach pulp	900 g/2 lb	tartaric acid	10 g/2 tsp
concentrated grape juice	250 g/9 oz	pectic enzyme and Campden tablets	
sugar	700 g/25 oz	Hock wine yeast and nutrient	

Liquidize the peach pulp, add 2.3 litres/4 pints cold water, one teaspoonful of acid, the pectic enzyme and one crushed Campden tablet. Cover and leave for 48 hours.

Strain the pulp through a fine meshed straining bag, drain it dry but do not press it.

Dissolve the sugar and remaining acid in 560 ml/1 pint of hot water and when it is cool, add it to the must.

Mix in an activated wine yeast and nutrient, pour the must into a demijohn, fit an airlock and ferment for four days.

Add the concentrated grape juice, top up and ferment out.

Rack into a storage jar, add one Campden tablet, seal and store until the wine is bright.

Siphon into bottles and add one saccharin tablet to each. Cork and keep for three months.

Serve this refreshing light, nearly dry wine well cooled on a warm day, preferably in the garden.

Pear wine

hard green pears	3 kg/6½ lb	Champagne wine yeast and nutrient	
sultanas	250 g/9 oz		
sugar	650 g/23 oz	*After 6 months:*	
tartaric acid	10 g/2 tsp	sugar	70 g/2½ oz
pectic enzyme and Campden tablets		Champagne wine yeast	

Cut off and discard the woody stalks and crush, mince or finely cut up the pears, dropping them at once into a bin containing 2 litres/3½ pints cold water, the pectic enzyme, acid and one crushed Campden tablet. Add the washed and chopped sultanas, cover and leave for 24 hours.

Mix in an activated Champagne wine yeast and nutrient, and

ferment on the pulp for five days, keeping the fruit submerged or pressed down twice daily.

Strain out, press dry and discard the fruit, stir in the sugar, pour the must into a demijohn, top up, fit an airlock, and ferment to dryness in an atmospheric temperature of 17°C/63°F.

Rack into a storage jar, seal and store in a cold place until the wine is bright, then rack again and keep for six months.

Check that the wine is dry (SG below 0.994), then mix in 70 g/2½ oz sugar and a second Champagne yeast. Fit an airlock and, as soon as the wine is fermenting, siphon it into six sterilized Champagne bottles. Fit hollow-domed plastic stoppers and wire cages, then store the bottles on their sides for a further six months.

See also page 98.

Pineapple wine

pineapple juice	1 litre/1¾ pints	pectic enzyme and Campden tablets
concentrated grape juice	250 g/9 oz	Burgundy wine yeast and nutrient
white sugar	1 kg/2¼ lb	
tartaric acid	10 g/2 tsp	

Boil the sugar and acid in 620 ml/21¾ fl oz water for 20 minutes, leave to cool, then store in a large bottle with a cork stopper.

Pour 2 litres/3½ pints of water into a demijohn, add the pineapple juice, concentrated grape juice, pectic enzyme and one Campden tablet. Seal and leave in a warm place for 24 hours.

Activate a sachet of wine yeast and nutrient in a cupful of water and mix it into the must, together with half the syrup, fit an airlock and ferment for a week in a cool place.

Mix in half the remaining syrup and one week later the rest. Top up with cold boiled water and ferment out.

Rack into a storage jar, top up, add one Campden tablet, seal and store until the wine is bright. Bottle and keep for three months, then serve cold as a dry aperitif, or sweeten it with saccharin to your taste.

Note: Some containers of juice hold more than 1 litre/1¾ pints. Any size from 1 to 1.25 litres is suitable. Reduce the water accordingly.

Plum wine 1

blue/black plums	2 kg/4½ lb	pectic enzyme and Campden tablets
sultanas	250 g/9 oz	
sugar	900 g/2 lb	Burgundy wine yeast and nutrient
grape tannin	5 g/1 tsp	

Wash the plums in hot water to remove any waxy bloom, place them in a bin and pour 3.4 litres/6 pints hot water over them. Cover and leave to cool.

Remove and discard the stones, add the washed and chopped sultanas, the pectic enzyme and one crushed Campden tablet. Cover and leave for 24 hours.

Activate the yeast in a cup of tepid water and mix it into the must with the nutrient and tannin.

Ferment on the pulp for four days, then strain out, press dry and discard the pulp. Stir in the sugar, pour the must into a demijohn, top up, fit an airlock and ferment out (21°C/70°F).

Rack into a storage jar, add one Campden tablet, seal and store until bright, then rack again and keep for one year.

Serve it free from chill with red meats or cheese.

Note: The colour and flavour can be enhanced by adding 200 g/7 oz of stalked, washed and crushed blackcurrants with the sultanas. Concentrated red grape juice could be used instead of sultanas.

Plum wine 2

Early River plums	2 kg/4½ lb	pectic enzyme & Campden tablets
concentrated grape juice	250 g/9 oz	Bordeaux wine yeast and nutrient
sugar	800 g/1¾ lb	

Wash the red, egg-shaped plums in hot water to remove any waxy bloom, place them in a bin and pour on 2.8 litres/5 pints hot water. Cover and leave to cool.

Remove and discard the stones, liquidize or crush the plums, add the pectic enzyme and one crushed Campden tablet. Cover and leave for 24 hours.

Dissolve the sugar in 560 ml/1 pint of hot water and leave to cool.

Strain out the plum pulp through a fine meshed nylon straining bag, roll the pulp around the bag to extract the juice, but do not press it.

Mix the sugar syrup, and activated yeast and nutrient into the must, pour it into a demijohn, fit an airlock and ferment for four days in a temperature around 19°C/66°F.

Mix in the concentrated grape juice, rosé or light red for preference, top up and ferment out.

Rack into a storage jar, add one Campden tablet, top up, seal and store until the wine is bright, then rack again. Keep for one year then bottle and slightly sweeten this rosé wine with saccharin.

Serve it cold with picnic sandwiches and party snacks.

Plum wine 3

canned plums	1.35 kg/3 lb	tartaric acid	5 g/1 tsp
concentrated grape juice	250 g/9 oz	pectic enzyme and Campden tablets	
sugar	800 g/1¾ lb	Hock wine yeast and nutrient	

Strain off and save the syrup. Remove and discard the stones, liquidize or crush the pulp, add 2.2 litres/4 pints water, the pectic enzyme and one crushed Campden tablet. Cover and leave for 24 hours.

Boil the sugar and acid in 560 ml/1 pint of water, leave to cool, bottle and seal.

Strain out the solids through a nylon sieve. Shake out as much juice as possible but do not press the pulp in case it is carried forward into the must.

Mix in the plum syrup and the sugar syrup, pour the must into a demijohn, add the activated yeast and nutrient, fit an airlock and ferment for four days, leaving a good air space in case of frothing.

Mix in the grape juice, top up with cold boiled water and leave the must to ferment out.

Rack into a storage jar, top up, add one Campden tablet, seal and store until the wine is bright, then bottle. Add one saccharin pellet to each bottle and serve this wine cold as soon as it is three months old.

Plum wine 4

yellow plums	2 kg/4½ lb	pectic enzyme and Campden tablets
sultanas	250 g/9 oz	Hock wine yeast and nutrient
sugar	800 g/1¾ lb	

Wash the plums in hot water to remove the bloom, remove and discard the stones then mash or liquidize the plums and sultanas. Place them in a bin with 3.4 litres/6 pints water, pectic enzyme and one crushed Campden tablet. Cover and leave for 24 hours.

Mix in the activated yeast and nutrient and ferment on the pulp for four days, keeping the fruit cap submerged.

Strain out, press dry and discard the pulp, stir in the sugar, pour the must into a demijohn, top up, fit an airlock and ferment out.

Rack into a storage jar, top up, add one Campden tablet, seal and store. When the wine is bright, rack again and keep for one year.

Sweeten to taste with saccharin and serve cold.

Plum wine 5

Victoria plums	2.25 kg/5 lb	pectic enzyme and Campden tablets
sultanas	250 g/9 oz	sherry flor yeast and nutrient
dried apricots	100 g/3½ oz	
sugar	1 kg/2¼ lb	

Wash the plums in hot water to remove the waxy bloom, then remove and discard the stones. Mash or liquidize the plums, the sultanas and the dried apricots. Place them all in a bin containing 2.8 litres/5 pints cold water, the pectic enzyme and one crushed Campden tablet. Cover and leave for 24 hours.

Activate the sherry flor yeast and add to the bin with the nutrient. Cover and ferment for four days, keeping the fruit cap submerged.

Dissolve the sugar in 560 ml/1 pint of hot water, leave to cool, then bottle, seal and store in the refrigerator until required.

Strain out, press dry and discard the pulp, mix in half the syrup, pour the must into a demijohn, fit an airlock and ferment for one week.

Mix in half the remaining syrup and one week later add the rest, then top up and leave to ferment out.

When the wine begins to clear, rack into a storage jar, seal and leave in a cold place. As soon as the wine is bright, rack into a larger container, mix in one bottle of fino sherry, and mature under an airspace protected with a plug of cotton wool.

After two years bottle and serve cold as a light, dry aperitif.

'Poor man's brandy'

crushed wheat	500 g/18 oz	grape tannin	2.5 g/½ tsp
old potatoes	1 kg/2¼ lb	yeast nutrient	5 g/1 tsp
chopped raisins	1 kg/2¼ lb	Benerva tablet (3 mg)	1
demerara sugar	1 kg/2¼ lb	cereal yeast	
large lemons	2	Tokay yeast	
tartaric acid	10 g/2 tsp		

Use old potatoes that are just beginning to sprout, but discard any that are green. Scrub off the dirt and when the skins are clean grate the potatoes into a bin containing the crushed wheat, washed and chopped raisins, and thinly pared lemon rind. Pour 2.8 litres/5 pints of hot water over them, cover and leave to cool.

Cut the lemons in halves, express all the juice and add this to the bin together with the activated cereal yeast, nutrient and Benerva tablet. Cover and ferment on the pulp in a warm place, 25°C/77°F, for five days, keeping the pulp submerged.

Boil the sugar and tartaric acid in 560 ml/1 pint of water for 20 minutes and leave to cool.

Strain out the wheat, raisins and lemon rind, press it dry, then discard it. Mix in half the syrup, the grape tannin and the activated Tokay yeast and pour the must into a demijohn; fit an airlock and continue the fermentation. After one week in a warm place, add half the remaining syrup, and one week later still, the rest. Top up the jar and leave the fermentation to finish.

When the wine begins to clear and all movement in the jar has stopped, rack into a storage jar, seal and leave in a cool place.

As soon as the wine is bright, rack again, top up, seal, label and store in a fairly inaccessible place for five years. Bottle and keep for a further year or two. Serve after the evening meal.

Prune wine

very large prunes	1 kg/2¼ lb	pectic enzyme and Campden tablets
sultanas	500 g/18 oz	
sugar	1 kg/2¼ lb	sherry yeast and nutrient
tartaric acid	10 g/2 tsp	

Wash the prunes, place them in a bin and pour 2.8 litres/5 pints hot water over them. Cover and leave overnight.

Next day, remove and discard the stones from the prunes, liquidize or chop the sultanas, and add these to the bin. Mix in the acid, pectic enzyme and one crushed Campden tablet. Cover and leave for 24 hours.

Add the activated sherry yeast and nutrient, and ferment for seven days, keeping the fruit cap submerged.

Boil the sugar with one teaspoonful of acid in 560 ml/1 pint of water for 20 minutes. Leave to cool then bottle, seal and store in the refrigerator until required.

Strain out, press dry and discard the pulp (or use it in a chutney), mix in half the sugar syrup, pour the must into a demijohn, fit an airlock and ferment for one week.

Mix in half the remaining syrup and one week later add the rest, top up and leave the must to ferment to a finish.

When the wine begins to clear, rack into two storage jars, leaving large air spaces in each, and plug the necks with cotton wool.

Rack as necessary, but mature the wine in this manner for at least one year, and preferably two. If you wish, you could mix in a bottle of Spanish sherry of a similar style (dry to medium) to fortify the flavour.

Raisin wine

raisins	2 kg/4½ lb	pectic enzyme and Campden tablets
brown sugar	250 g/9 oz	
tartaric acid	5 g/1 tsp	Madeira wine yeast and nutrient

Wash and chop, or liquidize the raisins, add 3.4 litres/6 pints water, pectic enzyme, acid and one crushed Campden tablet. Cover and leave for 24 hours.

Mix in an activated yeast and ferment on the pulp for ten days, keeping the fruit cap well submerged.

Strain out, press dry and discard the pulp, or mix it into a chutney, stir in the brown sugar, pour the must into a demijohn, top up, fit an airlock and finish the fermentation.

Rack into a storage jar, seal and store in a cold place until the wine is bright, then rack again and store in a very warm place (50°C/122°F) for at least three months. Return to a cool store for another year or so.

This strong wine then has the caramelized flavour of a Madeira wine and may be sweetened further if so desired.

Serve it cool with plain sponge cake.

Raspberry wine 1

raspberries	1 kg/2¼ lb	pectic enzyme and Campden tablets
sultanas	250 g/9 oz	
sugar	1 kg/2¼ lb	Bordeaux wine yeast and nutrient

Wash and crush the raspberries. Wash and chop the sultanas. Pour 2.8 litres/5 pints of cold water over them.

Mix in the pectic enzyme and one crushed Campden tablet, cover and leave for 24 hours.

Activate and mix in a Bordeaux wine yeast and some nutrient, then ferment on the pulp for four days, keeping the fruit submerged.

Dissolve the sugar in 560 ml/1 pint of hot water and when cool, bottle, seal and store in a refrigerator.

Strain out, press dry and discard the pulp, mix in half the sugar syrup, pour the must into a demijohn, fit an airlock, and leave for seven days.

Mix in half the remaining syrup and four days later, add the rest.

Ferment out, then rack and keep for at least one year. Bottle and keep for a further six months or longer.

Serve this wine slightly sweet, with one or two saccharin pellets per bottle.

Raspberry wine 2

raspberry jam	1.35 kg/3 lb	grape tannin	2.5 g/½ tsp
concentrated grape juice	250 g/9 oz	pectic enzyme and Campden tablets	
sugar	250 g/9 oz	Bordeaux wine yeast and nutrient	
tartaric acid	10 g/2 tsp		

Dissolve the jam in 3.4 litres/6 pints warm water and, when it is cooler, around 25°C/77°F, add a double dose of pectic enzyme, acid and one Campden tablet. Cover and leave for 24 hours.

Strain out the solids, mix in the grape juice, add the tannin, nutrient and activated yeast.

Pour the must into a demijohn, fit an airlock, and ferment for one week in a cool atmosphere just below 20°C/68°F.

Remove some must, stir in the sugar, return it to the jar, replace the airlock and ferment to a finish.

Rack into a storage jar containing a crushed Campden tablet, top up, seal and store until the wine is bright. Siphon into bottles and if the wine is too dry sweeten each bottle with one saccharin pellet.

Keep the wine for three months. Serve it cold with picnic sandwiches or party snacks.

Redcurrant wine 1

redcurrants	1 kg/2¼ lb	pectic enzyme and Campden tablets	
concentrated grape juice	250 g/9 oz	Bordeaux wine yeast and nutrient	
sugar	800 g/1¾ lb		

Stalk, wash and crush the redcurrants, pour on 3.4 litres/6 pints cold water, add the pectic enzyme and one crushed Campden tablet, cover and leave in a warm place for 24 hours.

Strain out the solids, press dry and discard them, stir in the sugar, pour the must into a demijohn, add an activated wine yeast and nutrient, fit an airlock, and ferment in a cool atmosphere, 18°C/64°F, for one week.

Mix in the concentrated grape juice (rosé for preference), top up and ferment out.

Siphon into a storage jar, add one Campden tablet, seal and store until the wine is bright, then rack again and store for one year.

Serve this attractive wine cold with picnic sandwiches and party snacks.

Redcurrant wine 2

redcurrant jelly	1.35 kg/3 lb	pectic enzyme and Campden tablets
concentrated grape juice	250 g/9 oz	Bordeaux wine yeast and nutrient
sugar	250 g/9 oz	
tartaric acid	5 g/1 tsp	

Dissolve the redcurrant jelly in 3.4 litres/6 pints warm water and, when it has cooled to about 25°C/77°F, add a double dose of pectic enzyme, the acid and one Campden tablet. Cover and leave for 24 hours.

Mix in the concentrated grape juice, nutrient and an activated yeast. Pour the must into a demijohn, fit an airlock and ferment for one week.

Remove some must, stir in the sugar, return it to the jar, top up with cold boiled water, replace the airlock and ferment to a finish.

Rack into a storage jar, add one Campden tablet, seal and store until the wine is bright, then bottle and keep for three months.

Serve this wine cold with picnic sandwiches and party snacks. Sweeten it slightly with saccharin if so desired.

Rhubarb wine

rhubarb	2.75 kg/6 lb	pectic enzyme and Campden tablets
sultanas	250 g/9 oz	Hock wine yeast and nutrient
sugar	800 g/1¾ lb	

Use red stalked rhubarb, freshly gathered in May or June. Cut off the leaf and the foot including a portion of stalk at both ends. Wash and crush or liquidize the stalks, or chop them into small pieces. Wash and chop or liquidize the sultanas.

Pour 2.8 litres/5 pints cold water on to the rhubarb and sultanas, then mix in the pectic enzyme and one crushed Campden tablet. Cover and leave for 24 hours.

Mix in an activated wine yeast and nutrient and ferment on the pulp for four days, keeping the fruit submerged, or gently pressed down twice each day.

Strain out, press dry and discard the pulp, stir in the sugar, pour the must into a demijohn, fit an airlock and ferment out.

Rack into a storage jar, add one Campden tablet, top up, seal and store until the wine is bright. Keep for one year and serve cold as a dry white wine.

Rosehip wine

ripe rosehips	1.35 kg/3 lb	pectic enzyme and Campden tablets
sultanas	250 g/9 oz	Sauternes wine yeast and nutrient
sugar	1 kg/2¼ lb	
citric acid	10 g/2 tsp	

Top, tail, wash and crush very ripe wild rosehips that have turned a deep orange colour. Place them in a bin with the washed and chopped sultanas and pour 3.4 litres/6 pints of boiling water over them. Cover and leave to cool.

Add the pectic enzyme, one teaspoonful of acid and one crushed Campden tablet, cover and leave for 24 hours.

Mix in the activated wine yeast and nutrient and ferment on the pulp for five days, keeping the fruit cap submerged.

Strain out, press dry and discard the pulp, and mix in the sugar and acid that has been boiled in one pint of water and allowed to cool.

Pour the must into a demijohn, fit an airlock and ferment to a finish.

Rack into a storage jar, add one Campden tablet, seal and keep for one year before bottling and then for a further three or four months.

Serve it cold and slightly sweet as a social wine.

Rosehip and fig wine

dried rosehip shells	250 g/9 oz	grape tannin	2.5 g/½ tsp
dried figs	200 g/7 oz	pectic enzyme and Campden tablets	
sultanas	250 g/9 oz	Tokay wine yeast and nutrient	
sugar	1.25 kg/2¾ lb		
tartaric acid	15 g/3 tsp		

Wash the rosehip shells, figs and sultanas, then break up the figs, chop the sultanas and place all these ingredients in a bin. Pour on 2.8 litres/5 pints of boiling water, cover and leave to cool.

Add the pectic enzyme, two teaspoonsful of acid and one crushed Campden tablet, cover and leave for 24 hours.

Mix in the activated wine yeast and nutrient, and tannin, then ferment on the pulp for four days, keeping the fruit cap submerged.

Boil the sugar with one teaspoonful of acid in 560 ml/1 pint of water for 20 minutes. Leave to cool, then bottle, seal and store in the refrigerator until required.

Strain out, press dry and discard the pulp, stir in half the sugar syrup, pour the must into a demijohn, fit an airlock and ferment for one week.

Mix in the rest of the syrup, top up and finish the fermentation.

Rack into a storage jar, add one Campden tablet and mature for 18 months in bulk and six months in bottle.

Serve this strong wine sweet and cold.

Rose petal wine

scented rose petals	1 litre/1¾ pints	sugar	250 g/9 oz
concentrated grape juice	1 kg/2¼ lb	Sauternes wine yeast	
		Campden tablet	

Place the rose petals in a suitable container, pour on 3.4 litres/6 pints boiling water and rub the petals against the side of the container with the back of a plastic spoon to extract the fragrant essences. Cover and leave to cool, but repeat this process several times.

Strain out, press dry and discard the petals, mix in the concentrated grape juice and an activated wine yeast, pour the must into a demijohn, fit an airlock and leave in a temperature around 18°C/64°F.

After ten days remove some must, stir in the sugar, return this to the jar, top up, replace the airlock and ferment to a finish.

Rack into a storage jar, add one Campden tablet, seal and store until the wine is bright, then bottle, sweeten to taste with saccharin, seal and store until the wine is six months old.

Serve it cool as a social wine.

Sloe wine

blue/black sloes	1.5 kg/3¼ lb	tartaric acid	5 g/1 tsp
raisins	250 g/9 oz	pectic enzyme and Campden tablets	
ripe bananas	4		
sugar	1.35 kg/3 lb	Port wine yeast and nutrient	

Stalk, and wash the sloes, place them in a bin and pour 2.5 litres/4½ pints of boiling water over them.

Peel and mash the bananas, wash and chop the raisins and add these to the bin.

Boil the sugar and acid in 1 litre/1¾ pints water, leave to cool, then bottle, seal and store in the refrigerator.

When the must is cool, add the pectic enzyme and one crushed Campden tablet. Cover and leave for 24 hours.

Mix in an activated yeast and nutrient, and ferment on the pulp for four days, keeping the fruit cap submerged.

Strain out, press dry and discard the pulp, mix in half the sugar syrup, pour the must into a jar, fit an airlock and leave in a warm place.

After one week, mix in half the remaining syrup and one week later the rest.

When fermentation is finished, rack the wine into a storage jar, seal and store until the wine is bright, then rack again.

Keep this wine in bulk for 18 months then bottle and keep for a further six months.

Serve it free from chill with cheese.

Sloe gin

very ripe sloes	340 g/12 oz
sugar	250 g/9 oz
gin	75 cl/26⅔ fl oz

Stalk, wash and prick the sloes with a sharp pointed fork or bodkin. Place them in a large kilner-type jar and sprinkle on the sugar. Mix in all the gin and seal the jar.

Shake the jar to dissolve the sugar and leave the jar where it can be available for shaking every other day for three months. This is necessary to extract the flavour from the sloes.

Strain out and gently press the sloes, pour the sloe gin into suitable bottles, seal and store for another nine months.

Serve as a liqueur after meals.

Sultana wine

sultanas	2kg/4½lb
citric acid	5g/1tsp
Sauternes wine yeast	

Wash and chop the sultanas, pour on 3.4 litres/6 pints cold water and mix in the acid and a Sauternes yeast.

Ferment on the pulp for ten days, keeping the fruit well submerged.

Strain out, press dry and discard the fruit, or use it in a chutney.

Pour the must into a demijohn, top up, fit an airlock and finish the fermentation.

Rack into a storage jar, add one Campden tablet, seal and store until the wine is bright.

Rack into bottles and keep for twelve months. Serve cold and slightly sweet.

Tropical fruit wine

tropical fruit juices	2 litres/3½ pints
pure grape juice	560 ml/1 pint
white sugar	800g/1¾lb
tartaric acid	5g/1tsp
pectic enzyme and Campden tablets	
Burgundy wine yeast and nutrient	

Pour the two cartons of tropical fruit juices and the bottle of grape juice into a demijohn, add the pectic enzyme and one crushed Campden tablet, seal and leave in a warm place for 24 hours.

Boil the acid and sugar in 1 litre/1¾ pints water and leave to cool.

Activate the yeast in 250 ml/8 fl oz of tepid water.

Mix in half the sugar syrup, the nutrient and the yeast, fit an airlock and ferment in a cool place for one week.

Add the rest of the syrup, top up and ferment out.

Rack into a storage jar, top up, add one Campden tablet, seal and store until the wine is bright.

Bottle and keep for three months, then serve cold as a dry wine or sweeten with saccharin to your taste.

Vine folly

vine prunings	2 kg/4½ lb	tartaric acid	15 g/3 tsp
grape juice	1 litre/1¾ pints	Hock wine yeast and nutrient	
white sugar	800 g/1¾ lb	Campden tablets	

Wash the vine shoots and leaves and chop them up into small pieces and then boil them in 3 litres/5¼ pints water in a covered preserving pan for half an hour.

Strain out and discard the folly, stir in the sugar and acid, then leave covered to cool.

Mix in the grape juice, activated yeast and nutrient, pour the must into a demijohn, top up, fit an airlock and ferment out.

Rack into a storage jar, add one Campden tablet, seal and store for two months, then rack again and keep for one year.

Serve this light white wine, nicely chilled and marginally sweetened with one or two saccharin tablets per bottle.

Wheat and raisin wine

crushed wheat	500 g/18 oz	tartaric acid	15 g/3 tsp
chopped raisins	500 g/18 oz	cereal wine yeast and nutrient	
sugar	1 kg/2¼ lb		

Pour 2.8 litres/5 pints boiling water over the wheat and raisins, cover and leave to cool.

Boil the sugar and 1 tsp acid and 560 ml/1 pint water for 20 minutes, leave to cool, then bottle, seal and store in the refrigerator.

Add 2 teaspoonsful acid to the must, together with an activated cereal yeast and nutrient.

Ferment on the pulp for four days, keeping the fruit cap well submerged.

Strain out, press dry and discard the pulp, stir in half the syrup, pour the must into a demijohn, fit an airlock and ferment in a temperature between 21–4°C/70–75°F.

After seven days, mix in half the remaining syrup and seven days later the rest.

When fermentation finishes, rack the wine into a storage jar, seal and store until the wine is bright, then rack again. Keep in bulk for eighteen months, then bottle and keep for a further six months. Serve it cool after meals. It should be strong and sweet.

Note: It is very important to use a cereal yeast since *Saccharomyces distaticus* is able to ferment at least some of the starch in the wheat as well as the sugar in the raisins and in the syrup.

Barley and raisin wine

The same quantity of pearl barley may be substituted for the wheat.

Rice and raisin wine

1 kg/2¼ lb crushed wholemeal rice may be substituted for the wheat.

Note: Cereal wines do benefit from long storage and continue to improve for up to five years.

Serving wine

Drinking wine from a bottle or even pouring it into a plastic beaker is not the best way to enjoy the results of your labours. Experience has shown that even wines of moderate or average quality can be enhanced by serving them in a sensible manner.

Maturity The first factor to observe is the maturity of the wine. A wine that has just finished fermenting, even an Express Kit Wine, will taste much better when it has had some time to mature. How long to keep a wine before drinking it depends on the wine itself. Each one varies. Wines that are light in body and alcohol, and wines made from kits or juices or canned fruits tend to mature more quickly than stronger, more full bodied or highly flavoured wines. The first category is often ready in three or four months, the second category may need three or four years. When bottling the second category it is sometimes helpful to use four standard size bottles and four half-size bottles. The latter can be drunk first at intervals of, say, two or three months. The improvement of the wine will become distinctly noticeable, and when the wine is fully mature there will still be four large bottles left. All too often it is found that the best bottle in a batch is the last.

Suitability The second factor to observe is the suitability of the wine for the occasion. A cream sherry or port style wine is not the best accompaniment with the main course of a meal. They can be better enjoyed afterwards. A dry or medium dry, less strong and less strongly flavoured wine will harmonize with the main course, but will be less attractive with the dessert course, or after the meal. So much extra pleasure can be obtained from wine by thoughtfully matching wine and food. In this context the experience of centuries of good living all over the world suggests dry red wines should be matched with red meats, game and cheese, and dry white wines with fish, pork or poultry. Sweet white wines are offered with the sweet course of a meal.

Temperature The temperature at which a wine is served is the next most important factor. There is no doubt that white wines are more appealing when they are served cool or even chilled: 10°C/50°F or just below is about right. This also applies to rosé wines, to sherry style and all aperitif wines, and especially to sparkling wines. Conversely, red wines taste best at room temperature, i.e. around 20°C/68°F. Apart from a few light red wines in the Beaujolais style, the tannin in red wines tastes bitter and harsh when the wine is cold but adds character to a wine at room temperature.

Decanters All home-made wines benefit from a period in a carafe or decanter before being served. Most of them are drunk far too young and a few hours in a decanter allows some acids and alcohols in the wine to combine with the oxygen in the air and form fragrant esters that enhance the bouquet and flavour of the wine. The decanter shows off the wine to its best effect if it is colourless and undecorated.

Glasses Similarly with glasses, the right type of glass for a wine improves the wine by its shape, retarding the bouquet by the inbuilt curve of the bowl or body. The glasses should be colourless and free from decoration. The bowl or body should be supported from a base by a stem that lifts it clear from the surface on which it is standing. It should be picked up by the stem and held by the base so as not to mask the wine with fingerprints or raise its temperature with a warm hand.

Quantity Wine glasses look best when they are only half to two-thirds full. Less than half looks mean, more than two-thirds looks greedy. Furthermore, it makes moving the glass difficult and smelling the bouquet impossible. Wine in a glass looks best on a white damask cloth or a silver salver. It looks less attractive on any highly coloured cloth or tray.

After use glasses and decanters should be washed in warm soapy water, thoroughly rinsed in cold and left to drain dry. They should be stored upright so that smells from the surface on which they stand are not entrapped in the glass.

Company There is little point in serving one of your best wines in the manner just described to someone who doesn't like wine and would perhaps prefer beer or a fruit squash. Consider the company, and to those who have not yet learned all the pleasures of wine, serve what they prefer. A famous judge, named Maurice Healy, wrote a most enjoyable book about wine in which he recommended, 'Serve your best wines to your best friends on your special occasions'. It is just as apt for homemade wines.

Drinking Finally, don't just gulp the wine, or use it solely 'to wash down the food'. Admire its clarity and colour in the glass, savour its aroma and bouquet, the fragrance of the ingredients and its complex vinosity. Taste the cleanliness and the balance of acidity, tannin, alcohol and flavour. Swallow the wine and wait for the farewell, or aftertaste, to register on your palate. Then talk about it: there are few activities in life more enjoyable than drinking wine in the best manner possible, and then talking about it with knowing friends.

But beware, alcohol can have unpleasant effects as well as enjoyable ones. Drink only with food and then but moderately. If you are driving afterwards restrict your drinking to just a half glass or two with your meal. Drink wine every day for your health's sake, but not so much that it damages your health. Half a bottle a day can be a tonic that keeps you well, relaxed and happy. A bottle or more per day could lead to disaster for you and those you love.

Meads

The oldest alcoholic drink known to mankind is no longer quite as popular as it once was. Honey is a relatively expensive ingredient today, although it is often available in supermarkets at no more than two-thirds the price of the honey in the health food shops. Any kind of honey may be used to make mead, but differently flavoured honeys produce differently flavoured meads.

Honey is made from the nectar of flowers and the varying perfumes are carried through to the finished mead. Beekeepers move their hives from one place to another as the blossoms appear so that their bees can gather specifically flavoured nectar. Perhaps the two best known of the imported honeys are Spanish orange blossom and Canadian clover. Both make superb meads but other types of honey can be used, especially in conjunction with other ingredients.

Mead has a taste that some people enjoy and others dislike. It is an acquired taste, for the flavour of most types of honey changes when the sugar is converted by fermentation into alcohol and carbon dioxide. To enjoy a particular honey is one pleasure, but to enjoy a mead made from that honey is quite a different matter. For this reason experience shows that mead is most popular when it is served slightly sweet, or at least not quite dry. Completely dry or very sweet meads have a very limited appeal.

Honey consists of approximately 77 per cent fermentable sugars, 17½ per cent water and the remaining 5½ per cent includes some salts of iron, phosphorous, lime, sodium, potassium, sulphur and manganese, with traces of citric, formic, malic, succinic and amino acids, dextrin, pollen, oils, gums, waxes, fats, yeasts, enzymes, vitamins, albumen, protein and ash. These quantities, although minute, vary slightly from honey to honey and account for the different flavours.

The acid content of honey is very low and sufficient acid must always be added to make an attractive mead. The quantity of nitrogen present is also negligible, so sufficient nutrient salts must be added to cause an effective fermentation.

Because honey contains some unwanted impurities for the making of mead – wild yeasts, gums, oils, wax, pollen etc. – it should be dissolved in warm water and then gently simmered for a few minutes. The impurities rise to the surface in the form of a scum that can be skimmed off. Keep the pan covered as much as possible and again while the must is cooling so that the dissipation of the volatile flavourings is kept to the minimum.

If you are a beekeeper, or have friendly access to one, the comb washings may also be used to make mead. After draining off as much honey as possible, wash the comb in as little hot water as is essential. Careful use of a clean sterilized brush would save immersing the entire comb in a container of water. When all the combs have had a first wash, they may be rinsed with fresh hot water into another container. Leave the liquors well covered while they cool, then measure their specific gravity. A light dry mead can be made from a honey solution with a specific gravity as low as 1.076. The comb washings may need adjusting slightly but should not be wasted. They, too, should be simmered for a few minutes so that the scum can be removed.

Honey can be used to make meads similar to all the wine styles and the methods are much the same. Perhaps the most successful are table mead made from orange blossom honey, and dessert mead made from clover honey with some leatherwood honey to enhance the flavour. Mead can be sparkled in the same way as wine, or oxidized and made into a sherry style wine. With long keeping the latter takes on a new flavour that is remarkably similar to sherry.

The following recipes are particularly successful.

Table mead

orange blossom honey	1.35 kg/3 lb	grape tannin	2.5 g/½ tsp
water	4 litres/7 pints	nutrient salts	5 g/1 tsp
acid blend*	20 g/4 tsp	Maury mead yeast	
		Campden tablet	

*Acid blend is a mixture of tartaric, malic and citric acids usually obtainable from the specialist Home Brew shops. You can mix it yourself in the proportion of 3:2:1 in the order mentioned. Any of the acids may be used alone if you prefer.

Prepare the honey as already indicated and when the must is cool enough, 21°C/70°F, mix in the acid, tannin, nutrient salts and an activated yeast.

Pour the must into a demijohn, fit an airlock and ferment out. This may take two weeks or two months. Honey fermentations are variable in length.

Rack into a storage jar, top up, add one Campden tablet and mature the mead for at least one year, racking as may be necessary.

Serve this mead chilled with cold chicken, smoked salmon, or mousse. Alternatively, it makes an attractive aperitif since it contains the subtle perfume of orange blossom.

Taste the mead dry and if need be ameliorate each bottle with a rounded teaspoonful of honey or with one saccharin pellet just before serving.

Dessert mead

clover honey	1.35 kg/3 lb	grape tannin	2.5 g/½ tsp
leatherwood honey	450 g/1 lb	nutrient salts	5 g/1 tsp
water	3.7 litres/6½ pints	Sauternes wine yeast	
acid blend	25 g/5 tsp	Campden tablet	

Prepare the clover honey in approximately 2.8 litres/5 pints of water in the manner already described. Mix in the acid, tannin, nutrient and yeast and ferment in a demijohn under an airlock.

After one week, prepare the leatherwood honey in the remaining water and when it is cool remove the airlock and mix it in to the fermenting must. Replace the airlock and continue the fermentation to the end.

Rack into a storage jar, top up, add one Campden tablet and keep for two years, racking when necessary.

Serve this stronger and sweeter mead cool with shortbread biscuits.

Other meads

Mead-makers of former centuries used to vary the flavour of their beverage with fruits, flowers, herbs and spices. These can be quickly imitated today merely by adding some honey instead of sugar to any of the wine recipes. You have only to remember that 454 g/1 lb of honey contains only 340 g/12 oz sugar. In most recipes this is an adequate addition of honey and does not overwhelm the other flavours. Some of these mixtures have specific names, for example:

Ciser is a mixture of cream set honey and apple juice.

Pyment is a mixture of honey and grape juice. Use cream set honey with white grapes.

Melomel is a mixture of honey and other fruits or flowers. Use cream set honey with white fruits and all flowers.

Metheglin is a mixture of honey and herbs or spices. Loose brown honey may be used.

Hypocras is a mixture of honey, grape juice and herbs or spices. Use cream set or loose brown honey.

When making any of the herb or spice flavoured meads it is best not to overdo the flavourings. A bouquet garni of herbs or spices suspended in the fermenting must for two or three days is usually adequate. Furthermore, because of the presence of the herbs or spices it is essential, in the author's opinion, to serve these meads fairly sweet, but not cloyingly so. Spiced and herbal meads make superb sweetened mulls on a cold night. Warm them slowly to 60°C/140°F and drink them from a warm glass. They are not only enjoyable, but also good for you.

Sparkling mead is best made from 1.35 kg/3 lb of blended cream set honey purchased from a supermarket. Make the mead as described for table purposes but when it is six months old, quite dry (SG lower than 1.000), and crystal clear, mix in 100 g/3½ oz honey together with a champagne yeast and a little nutrient. When fermentation starts pour the mead into champagne bottles and seal them with hollow-domed plastic stoppers wired on with cages.

Sherry style mead can be made from loose brown honey in the same manner as described for a dessert mead, but use a sherry wine yeast and add one 3 mg Benerva tablet with the nutrient. The specific gravity of the must should be checked at regular intervals and the second honey solution should be added in small doses every few days. But do not start the additions until the specific gravity of the first honey solution has fallen to 1.002.

When fermentation of the whole must is finished, the mead should be racked, but not topped up nor sulphited. The neck of the jar should not be sealed, but merely plugged with cotton wool. Maturation takes a long time and this mead should preferably be labelled and stored in some fairly inaccessible place where it can be forgotten for five years or longer.

Cider

One of our oldest beverages, as popular in Biblical days as in the days of the Druids in England. Valued more in seventeenth-century London than imported wine from France, then discarded in favour of the improved beer, and the new drinks of tea, coffee and gin. Now cider is back in favour. A delicate flavoured, light bodied, cool and thirst quenching drink.

Cider from a 'kit' Cider kits similar to wine kits and beer kits can be bought. The concentrated French cider-apple juice is packed in various sized containers and needs only some water, sugar and yeast to ferment it into 16, 24 or 32 pints. The method is much the same as for making wine. After sterilizing a suitable container, the concentrate, water and sugar are mixed together. An activated yeast is then added and the cider is fermented under an airlock to dryness. After racking and clearing, the cider is bottled and kept for a few weeks to mature.

Alternatively, you can sweeten the cider to taste with saccharin or pour it into a plastic beer keg and carbonate it slightly with a CO_2 injector. The result is a sparkling, as opposed to a still cider. Sometimes the sparkling ciders taste better when they are not too dry and you may find that one saccharin pellet per pint improves their flavour.

This is the quick, easy way to make cider but it lacks any touch of craftsmanship and the satisfaction that accompanies the making of a beverage from the base ingredient.

Real cider Cider apples can often be obtained from local farmers in the West of England. There are many cider orchards in that area and a polite request at the right time is likely to be well received. You may even find some orchards where you can 'pick your own' cider apples for a reasonable price.

Preparation It is important to get a selection of sweet, sharp and bitter apples roughly in the proportion of 4:2:1. To make one gallon of cider you will need 10 kg/22 lb of apples, possibly even a few more if the fruit is not very juicy. Before use, the apples should be mellowed in a cool store for about three weeks, if possible in trays rather than in piles. By this time they will be softer but still quite hard and you will most certainly need some means of crushing them and pressing them dry. Proper equipment becomes more important when you think about the quantity of cider you want to make – five gallons is soon drunk!

Crushing For the crushing you could use a stainless steel blade attached to a stainless steel shaft which can be passed through the lid of a bin into an electric drill. Wash the apples, quarter them into the bin until it is about half to two thirds full, then fit the lid containing the shaft and move the blade up and down and around in the bin for about a minute, then check on the size of the pieces in your mash. The smaller the pieces the easier will be the pressing, but beware of oxidation, i.e. browning of the fruit. As soon as possible add one 5 ml teaspoonful of a 10 per cent solution of sulphite for every 4 kg/9 lb apples being crushed. A similar spoonful of a pectic enzyme should also be added.

Pressing When the apples are adequately pulped, empty them into a freshly sterilized nylon straining bag already fitted into a press that can drain through a funnel into a demijohn. If you have someone to help you, one person could continue to prepare the apples and crush them while the other pressed the pulp. In these circumstances the sulphite and pectic enzyme could be placed in the receiving jar as soon as the juice begins to flow.

To extract the maximum juice from the pulp, the pressure should be steadily increased to the maximum and held there until the juice ceases to flow. Release the pressure, open the bag, and stir up the pulp. Alternatively, turn the bag upside down. Reinstate the maximum pressure and the juice will flow again in surprising abundance. When the flow ceases, again open the bag and stir up the pulp or just turn the bag on to its side. Once more the juice will flow. Repeat this once more and the pulp will then be in the form of a firm 'cake' that you can lift out in one piece.

From 10 kg/22½ lb of apples a demijohn should now be full of juice. Seal the jar and leave it in a cool place for 24 hours. If there is a heavy sediment of fruit pulp in the jar, rack off the clearer juice and filter out the pulp from the remainder.

Fermentation The specific gravity of the must should now be checked and a reading between 1.046 and 1.050 is the optimum. If the reading is lower than this, mix a little sugar into say 250 ml/9 fl oz of juice and add to the bulk. The reading in 4.5 litres/1 gallon of juice will be raised 5 units by 55 g/2 oz of sugar.

An activated yeast should now be added. Commercial cider makers use *Saccharomyces cerevisiae uvarum*, but this is not yet widely available, and a champagne wine yeast is equally suitable. It would contribute to the ultimate clarity of your cider if you were also to include one level teaspoonful of soluble bentonite. Then fit an airlock and once fermentation has started, move the jar to a cooler place for a long, slow ferment rather than a hasty one at a higher temperature. The cooler ferment better retains the delicate flavours of the apples.

Maturation When fermentation is finished and the cider begins to clear, rack it into a storage jar, top it up with other cider or cold boiled water, add 50 ppm of sulphite and leave it in the coldest place you can find until it is bright. If you have an efficient filter kit, the cider may well be sufficiently clear at the end of a slow and cool fermentation to be racked through a filter direct into screw-stoppered bottles. These should then be labelled and stored upright in a cool dark place for three or four months while the cider matures.

Should you have the good fortune to be able to make several batches of cider during the season, they should all be subsequently blended together. When all the batches are clear siphon them into a large enough container that has just been sterilized. Wash out and sterilize the smaller containers and refill them or bottle the blended cider. Commercial ciders are always blended and experience of making cider in the home shows that blending improves the flavour. Before mixing one cider with another, however, do check by smell and taste that each one is sound and there is no trace of vinegar or bacterial infection in any of them. Never mix an unsound cider with a good one because the infection will spoil it.

Screw-stoppered bottles are used for cider because long storage is not necessary. Sometimes a little liveliness may develop from the conversion of some of the malic acid into lactic acid and carbon dioxide. It is best to use the brown screw-stoppered cider bottles, carbonated mineral water bottles or beer bottles.

Cider from other apples

Many people are unable to obtain proper cider apples and may have to use the best they can get. Some excellent ciders have been made from these other apples, but it is important to remember the proportion of four measures of sweet apples to two measures of sharp apples and one measure of bitter apples. That splendid cooking apple, the Bramley, is not really suitable for cider because it is so very sharp. The actual varieties that you use may be a matter of choice, or more likely, what is available to you. For bitter apples you could use John Downie crab apples or the Siberian red or yellow varieties. A few hard pears would also add a little tannin.

When making cider from other than cider apples, it is worthwhile including some concentrated cider-apple juice. A suitable recipe for 13.5 litres/3 gallons is as follows:

sweet apples	9 kg/20 lb	sugar (if necessary)
sharp apples	4.5 kg/10 lb	pectic enzyme and sulphite
crab apples	2.5 kg/6 lb	bentonite
concentrated cider juice	1 kg/2¼ lb	Champagne wine yeast and nutrient

Dissolve the concentrated cider apple juice (sufficient for 9 litres/16 pints) in 4.5 litres/1 gallon water and add the 3 teaspoonsful pectic enzyme, three crushed Campden tablets or the equivalent. Wash, crush and press the apples as quickly as you can and allow the juice to run into the container of diluted concentrated cider apple juice. If necessary, make up to 13.5 litres/3 gallons. Check the specific gravity and if necessary make up to 1.050.

Cover and leave for 24 hours, then add the activated yeast and 3 level 5 ml spoonsful of soluble bentonite. Fit an airlock and ferment out in a cool place.

Rack into a storage jar or jars, top up and sulphite at the rate of 50 ppm. Seal and keep for four months, then bottle into screw-stoppered beer or cider bottles. Keep for a further month or so then chill and serve cool with all ham and bacon meals.

PROBLEMS

The main faults found in cider are:

- acetification
- oxidation
- lack of flavour
- haziness.

Acetification This can be recognized by a faint or pronounced vinegar smell and sometimes taste. It is caused by using damaged fruit that has been infected with *Mycoderma aceti*, by the tiny fruit fly that seems to appear almost from nowhere whenever over-ripe or damaged fruit is about. The problem can be prevented by examining your fruit carefully and discarding damaged fruit or at least by cutting out all damaged parts.

If during the making process you leave fruit or must uncovered and/or unprotected with sulphite, then you must also expect this trouble.

There is no known cure. If the smell of vinegar is not too strong you can drink the cider yourself, but don't offer it to other people! If the infection is severe, the cider could be turned into vinegar for culinary use. Simply add 1 litre/1¾ pints of bought vinegar to 5 litres/9 pints of your acetified cider and leave the 6 litres/10¾ pints in a container suitable for at least 12 litres/3 gallons. Plug the neck loosely with a small quantity of cotton wool or paper tissue. Leave the container in a warm and airy place for three months, while the alcohol is converted into acetic acid. Then siphon the vinegar into bottles and sterilize it. A large stewpan, preserving pan or fish kettle will do for this. Place some thin wooden slats or a thick cloth on the bottom of the vessel, stand the loosely stoppered bottles on this, fill the pan with water to the neck of the bottles, place on the heat and boil the water for 20 minutes. This effectively sterilizes the vinegar, so screw down the stoppers and when the bottles are cool check the stoppers again. The cider vinegar will be ready for use within a month or so.

Oxidation When apples are cut and exposed to the air, the surface becomes brown. Bramley apples are notorious for this and go brown in a few seconds. Other apples are a little slower to change colour. If you eat fruit that contains an area of this brown part the taste is affected and the flavour is dulled or flattened. If you try to make cider from apples that contain brown, bruised or damaged portions or surfaces, this flavour will be carried over and the result will be a 'brown and flat' taste. It is very important then to prepare and crush your fruit and handle your juice so that it is not so exposed to the air that it has time to turn brown. After washing your apples, they can be cut up into smaller portions for the crushing process and dropped into water containing 50 ppm of sulphite. When you are ready to crush them, remove them from the water, shake off the surplus moisture and place them in your bin. Try to press out the juice immediately after crushing, but if this is not possible, place the pulp in a container and cover it with a cloth that has been dipped in a sulphite solution and wrung out. Lay the cloth directly on to the pulp so as to exclude as much air as possible.

After pressing the pulp, keep the juice, and subsequently the cider, well protected with sulphite in vessels that are full, well-sealed, and covered with material that keeps out the light. All this ensures that the cider will be a good colour and free from the taint of oxidation. There is not much use for a heavily oxidized cider.

Lack of flavour In a dull and wet season, fruits often lack flavour and if you have to use fruits that are low in flavour there is not much that you can do about it. Do your best to include as many strong-flavoured eating apples in your recipe as you can. These apples may not be available to you throughout the season. Depending on your facilities you can either blend together several different batches of cider at the end of the season, or you could prepare and freeze those strong flavoured apples for use at a later date. Frozen apples are as good as fresh when thawed, but do thaw them in a sulphite solution to avoid oxidation.

Haziness Sometimes a cider is slow to clear and this may be due to pectin or protein. You can check for a pectin haze as already described on page 46 and cure it with a dose of a fresh pectic enzyme. A protein haze used to be cleared with milk, but nowadays it is more customary to use casein or bentonite. If you add pectic enzyme 24 hours before adding the yeast and bentonite with the yeast, your cider will clear quickly and you will have no problems with haze.

Serving cider

It is important to remember that cider is often stronger than beer. It should be treated with respect. It tastes best when it is only slightly chilled. No more than one hour in a refrigerator is sufficient. It tastes good by itself, but is the perfect companion for a ham sandwich. Indeed cider accompanies ham in all its forms. Ham and bacon cuts should be baked or boiled in cider, or at least in water to which cider has been added. Use cider to make a summer cup or a winter punch. Be imaginative with it.

Glossary for beer-making

adjuncts Beer is made from malt, hops, water and yeast. All other items included in a recipe are adjuncts. They include sugar, flakes, syrups and other cereals.
CO_2 injector An instrument that can be fitted to a plastic pressure barrel or keg from which draught beer is to be dispensed. The instrument holds a bulb containing carbon dioxide under pressure. When the plunger is pressed a measured amount of carbon dioxide is injected into the barrel. This keeps the remaining beer in good condition after some has been drawn off.
condition The liveliness or lack of it in a beer. A beer in good condition has a steady bead of carbon dioxide bubbles rising to the surface, but is not too gassy. A beer in bad condition is still and flat, with a dull taste.
dextrins Sugars produced during mashing that are very difficult for yeast to ferment. They give body and a hint of sweetness to a beer.
finings A substance added to a beer to help it clear quickly. There are two kinds. One, sometimes called Irish moss, is added while the wort and hops are being boiled. The other is added when fermentation is finished. There are a number of proprietary brands available for use in accordance with the instructions given on the package. Most beers clear by themselves, but it is sometimes helpful to add finings to draught beers.
goods/grist The collective name for all the dry malts, cereals and flakes that go into the mashing vessel.
hardening salts A mixture of mineral salts, including calcium sulphate and magnesium sulphate, that can be added to soft water to make it more suitable for brewing bitter beers and barley wines.
head The froth on the top of a glass or tankard of beer. It consists of bubbles of carbon dioxide created by a secondary fermentation and held together by constituents in the beer.

hops The flower cone of the vine *Humulus lupulus* used for flavouring and preserving beer.
Irish moss/carragheen moss A fining agent used during the boiling of the hops to help clarify the wort prior to yeasting.
liquor The name brewers use for water.
malt After water, malt is the main ingredient in the brewing of beer. It is made by germinating barley grains in a moist, warm armosphere and then roasting them to a lesser or greater degree.
malt extract/syrup A toffee-like substance made by concentrating the solution produced when malted barley is mashed/steeped in hot water for several hours.
mash The action used to describe the conversion of the starch in malted barley to maltose by steeping it in hot water for several hours. The word mash is also used to describe the mixture of grains, adjuncts and water.
prime The addition of some unfermented wort or a small amount of sugar to a fully fermented wort in order to create a further fermentation in a sealed bottle or cask and so condition a beer.
rouse To stir-up a fermenting wort after skimming off the scum. The wort at the bottom of the bin must be brought up to the top. A slightly different action from merely stirring.
scum The dirty froth that develops on the surface of a fermenting wort. It must be removed so that it does not spoil the flavour of the beer.
wort The name given to the solution that is to be fermented into beer.
yeast In brewing, the single-celled fungus *Saccharomyces cerevisiae* is used for most beers, but the variety known as *Saccharomyces carlsbergensis* is used for lagers. Many brewers just refer to brewer's yeast as opposed to baker's yeast which has a doughy flavour.

Brewing at home

Beer has been brewed in the homes of Britons for more than two thousand years, for most of that time by women. Only for the past three centuries have men and breweries been involved. Nowadays, beer is brewed in the homes of at least one of every six families. Mostly, it must be admitted, from the wide range of kits that are so readily available in places like specialist home brew shops, Boots the Chemist, Woolworth's, supermarkets, do-it-yourself and garden centres.

You can choose not only the style of beer you prefer, bitter, brown, stout, lager or barley wine, but a size of kit to suit your capacity and facilities, from 16 to 40 pints. Most kits are wet, i.e. they consist of a container of toffee-like malt extract that has been flavoured with hop essence. You have only to provide the water and some sugar. A sachet of yeast granules is usually included, together with step-by-step instructions. But a few kits are dry, i.e. they consist of a sealed bag of malt flour, together with another of hops and grains. Yeast granules and detailed instructions are also provided and again, you have only to provide the water and some extra sugar.

A criticism that can be made of nearly all these kits is that too much sugar is required. Sugar can readily be converted into alcohol, but this thins the beer and diminishes the malty flavour. The manufacturers of some kits recognize this fault and suggest that you reduce the water content if you want to increase the malty flavour.

But doing this increases the hop flavour and the balance of the beer becomes maladjusted.

Nevertheless, it must be recognized that millions of people are satisfied with the beer that they brew from the kits that they buy. The equipment required for brewing these beers is minimal and the process of brewing them is quick and easy. Within three weeks from starting the brew it is ready for drinking, although it improves if kept for several weeks longer.

For those who have never made beer before, it is a good introduction to brewing at home to begin with a small size wet kit. Good hygiene is important and you must start by sterilizing your container with a sulphite solution. The malt extract must then be dissolved in the specified amount of water and the sugar stirred in. Some instructions then recommend the boiling of this wort, as the solution is called, for five minutes. Cold water is then added to make up to the stated quantity, and when the temperature of the wort has fallen to 20°C/68°F the yeast granules are sprinkled on. The container is covered and left while fermentation takes place. As soon as it is finished, the beer is siphoned into freshly sterilized bottles, primed with sugar, sealed and stored for a minimum of five days. It should be cooled before serving.

The more adventurous and those with a little more time, having mastered this simple activity, may prefer to brew beers that are more specific to their particular palate and in the true tradition of brewing from malted grains, adjuncts and hops. This process, however, requires the mashing or steeping of the crushed grains in hot water at a controlled temperature for two hours or more, then the sparging (see page 146), or washing, of the grains with more hot water and finally the long boiling of the wort and hops. At first, the process seems daunting and off-putting.

There is a middle way, however. You can buy containers of concentrated malt syrup for the particular purposes of brewing the main beer styles. In the manufacture of these syrups the malted barleys have been carefully blended to produce what the manufacturer's head brewer regards as the correct wort. Each brewer has his own opinion as to the best formula. It may not coincide with yours, and you should try all the brands until you have found the one you like best. The dilution of this syrup with water saves you the trouble of selecting the most suitable grains, crushing, mashing and sparging them.

Now you can vary the wort to suit yourself. You can experiment with the inclusion of various adjuncts including rice, maize, barley and wheat in the form of flakes, torrified barley, or wheat flour. A type of syrup can be bought still containing some 'diastase' enzymes that will convert the starch in your adjuncts into maltose. It is called diastatic malt syrup, or just DMS.

You can also choose your hops – the traditional Golding, Fuggle or Northern Brewer varieties, or the newer developments from Wye Agricultural College in Kent: Challenger, Northdown or Target. For lager style beer you should use the Continental Hallertau, Saaz or Styrian hops.

Sugar also provides you with choice and, in addition to granulated white sugar, you could use some brown sugar, golden treacle, even a tablespoonful of black treacle, glucose in the form of lumps called chips or as a white powder, or invert sugar – preferably made yourself.

You can also control the ratio of sugar to malt and keep it to no more than half, and preferably to a third or even a quarter. Finally, you decide on the strength of your beer, although there is no merit in a strong beer unless it is properly balanced in body and flavour. There are hundreds of variations and the following recipes are but a few to point the way.

Beer recipes

The metric and imperial quantities are so close to each other that it doesn't matter which are used. In the United Kingdom the Government has declared its intention of preserving the pint measure and, therefore, the gallon (8 pints).

Many ingredients are marketed, however, in metric quantities and some suppliers equate the ounce with 25 grams, while others offer 30 grams. The difference makes no significant variation in the beers.

If the hops called Challenger, Northdown and Target are not available in your local shops, use Goldings, Fuggles and Northern Brewer instead, but use about a quarter more since the old varieties contain less alpha acid than the newer ones. Pellets are highly concentrated but their equivalent of the natural hop is usually indicated.

The quantities given may be varied up or down, pro rata, to suit your facilities. The recipes given are offered primarily for guidance and may be varied to suit your requirements.

Don't forget the importance of good hygiene and the need for good quality ingredients. Finally, do give the beers an adequate chance to mature before you drink them.

Bitter beer 1

malt syrup	900 g/2 lb	Challenger hops	25 g/1 oz
golden syrup	450 g/1 lb	beer yeast	

Boil the hops in 2 litres/3½ pints of water for 20 minutes in a covered pan.

Pour 2 litres/3½ pints hot water into a fermentation bin and dissolve in it the two syrups. Wash out each container with a little more hot water so that no syrup is wasted.

Strain the hop water into the bin, add another 2 litres/3½ pints of water to the hops and boil them a second time for 20 minutes.

Strain this water into the bin, discard the hops, add sufficient cold water to make the total up to 9 litres/15¾ pints, cover and leave to cool.

Sprinkle the dried yeast granules on to a cupful of tepid water (40°C/104°F) and leave them to rehydrate.

Stir the activated yeast into the wort, cover loosely and leave in a cool position (18°C/64°F) for about six days.

On the second and third days skim off the froth and rouse up the beer.

When the surface of the beer is clear and still, siphon it into sterilized bottles, prime with granulated sugar at the rate of half a level 5 ml spoonful per 560 ml/1 pint, seal and store for three weeks. (Makes about 9.5 litres/16 pints.)

Bitter beer 2

malt syrup	900 g/2 lb	Challenger hops	25 g/1 oz
flaked maize	56 g/2 oz	beer yeast	
light brown sugar	340 g/12 oz		

Boil the hops in 2 litres/3½ pints of water for 20 minutes.

Pour 2 litres/3½ pints of hot water into a fermentation bin, dissolve the malt syrup in it and rinse out the container with a little more water.

Sprinkle on and stir in the flaked maize.

Strain the hop water into the bin, add another 2 litres/3½ pints and boil the hops for a further 20 minutes. Strain this into the bin and discard the hops.

Stir in the sugar, cover and leave to cool.

Rehydrate the yeast in a cup of tepid water.

Strain out the flaked maize, add sufficient cold water to make the total up to 9 litres/15¾ pints, then stir in the yeast.

Ferment the wort in a cool atmosphere, skimming and stirring on the second and third days.

Bottle, prime, seal and store as already directed. (Makes about 9.5 litres/16 pints.)

Draught bitter

malt syrup	1.8 kg/4 lb	Challenger hops	56 g/2 oz
crystal malt grains	340 g/12 oz	Target hops	15 g/½ oz
flaked maize	85 g/3 oz	beer yeast	
white sugar	900 g/2 lb		

Dissolve the malt syrup in at least 4.5 litres/1 gallon of warm water, mix in the crystal malt grains, flaked maize and Challenger hops.

Boil vigorously for 30 minutes, then add the Target hops and continue the boil for another 15 minutes. Leave to cool for 15 minutes.

Strain out the solids, rinse them in 1 litre/1¾ pints of hot water, then discard them.

Stir in the sugar, make up the total wort to 22.5 litres/5 gallons with cold water and, when cool, mix in an activated beer yeast.

Skim and rouse on the second and third days, then leave to ferment out in a cool place.

Siphon into a pressure keg, stir in 70 g/2½ oz priming sugar, seal and store for at least ten days.

When the condition of the beer deteriorates, add CO_2 or reprime the beer and leave it for a further ten days. (Makes about 22.5 litres/ 5 gallons.)

India pale ale

pale malt syrup	900 g/2 lb	flaked barley	56 g/2 oz
crystal malt grains	100 g/3½ oz	white sugar	250 g/9 oz
golden syrup	100 g/3½ oz	Challenger hops	25 g/1 oz
flaked rice	56 g/2 oz	beer yeast	

Dissolve the pale malt syrup in 2 litres/3½ pints hot water and mix in the flaked rice and flaked barley.

Boil the crystal malt grains and all but a small handful of hops for 30 minutes, then strain the liquor into the wort. Add 2 litres/3½ pints of water to the hops and boil for a further quarter of an hour. Strain this liquor into the wort, discard the solids, cover the wort and leave to cool.

Strain out the flaked rice and flaked barley, mix in the golden syrup and white sugar, then top up to the 9 litre/2 gallon level with cold water. Add a beer yeast activated in a cup of tepid water, and ferment in a cool atmosphere.

Skim and rouse on the second and third days, then mix in the remaining hops.

When fermentation is finished, siphon into bottles, prime, seal and store for six weeks. (Makes about 9 litres/16 pints.)

Lager

lager malt syrup	900 g/2 lb	water	8 litres/14 pints
flaked rice	56 g/2 oz	table salt	2 g/⅓ tsp
white sugar	280 g/10 oz	lager yeast	
Hallertau hops	25 g/1 oz		

Boil all but a small handful of the hops in 2 litres/3½ pints of water for 20 minutes.

Dissolve the lager malt syrup in 2 litres/3½ pints of hot water, add the salt and the flaked rice. Strain the hop liquor on to the wort, and stir well.

Add 2 litres/3½ pints of water to the hops, boil again for 20 minutes, strain the liquor into the wort, discard the hops, cover the wort and leave to cool.

Strain out the rice, stir in the sugar, add cold water to the wort to a total of 9 litres/2 gallons, then mix in the lager yeast reactivated in a cup of tepid water.

Next day, skim off any scum that may have arisen, mix in the remaining hops, wetting them thoroughly, stir up the wort, replace the cover and move the bin to a cooler place for a longer and slower fermentation. An atmospheric temperature around 12°C/54°F is best.

When fermentation is finished, bottle, prime, seal and store for three months. (Makes about 9 litres/16 pints.)

Barley wine

malt syrup	1.35 kg/3 lb	citric acid	2.5 g/½ tsp
crystal malt	100 g/3½ oz	Challenger hops	20 g/¾ oz
brown sugar	200 g/7 oz	Champagne wine yeast	

Heat about 3.4 litres/6 pints water in a preserving pan then slowly stir in the malt syrup ensuring that it is well dissolved and that none settles on the bottom and burns.

Add the crystal malt grains and half the hops, and boil for 30 minutes. Add the remaining hops and continue boiling for a further 15 minutes.

Cover the pan and leave to cool for 15 minutes. Strain out the hops and grains and discard them, stir in the sugar and acid, then cover and leave to cool.

Activate a champagne wine yeast in half a cup of tepid water, add to the wort, stir well and increase the volume of wort to 4.5 litres/ 1 gallon.

Ferment in an atmosphere around 17°C/63°F, skimming on the second day if necessary and rousing gently. The wort could then be transferred to a demijohn and finished off under an airlock. The original gravity of the wort will be around 1.100 and the finishing gravity around 1.015. The alcohol content will then be at least 11 per cent!

Bottle this wine in half pints and prime each one with only a quarter teaspoonful of sugar. Seal and store for at least twelve months, then serve in wine glasses – not tankards! (Makes about 4.5 litres/8 pints.)

Stout (dry)

malt syrup	900 g/2 lb	table salt	1 g/¼ tsp
brown sugar	340 g/12 oz	Northdown hops	25 g/1 oz
roast barley	56 g/2 oz	beer yeast	
black malt	56 g/2 oz		

Boil the hops, roast barley and black malt in 2 litres/3½ pints water for 20 minutes.

Strain the liquor into a bin containing the malt syrup, sugar and salt dissolved in 2 litres/3½ pints hot water.

Add another 2 litres /3½ pints of water to the hops, boil for a further

20 minutes, then strain the liquor into the bin and discard the hops and grains.

Make up the total wort to 9 litres/2 gallons and, when cool, siphon 425 ml/15 fl oz of the wort into a sterilized bottle, seal and store in the refrigerator.

Mix in a beer yeast that has been activated in a cupful of tepid water, loosely cover and leave in a cool atmosphere.

Skim and stir on the second and third days and, when fermentation is finished, move the bin to a cold place for a few days, or rack the beer into two demijohns, seal and leave on a stone floor for two or three days to encourage the clarification.

Distribute the unfermented wort evenly among the bottles, siphon in the beer, seal and store for three weeks. (Makes about 9 litres/16 pints.)

Stout (sweet)

malt syrup	900 g/2 lb	Northdown hops	20 g/¾ oz
black malt	56 g/2 oz	table salt	1 g/¼ tsp.
flaked barley	56 g/2 oz	lactose	200 g/7 oz
brown sugar	200 g/7 oz	beer yeast	

Boil the hops, black malt and flaked barley for 30 minutes in 2 litres/3½ pints of water.

Dissolve the malt syrup, brown sugar and salt in a further 2 litres/3½ pints hot water.

Strain on the hop liquor and discard the solids.

Make up to 9 litres/2 gallons with cold water and leave to cool.

Stir in a yeast that has been activated in a cupful of tepid water and ferment in a cool atmosphere.

Skim and stir on the second and third days and, when fermentation has finished, rack into a clean vessel. Stir in the lactose and 8 level 5 ml spoonsful of sugar.

Siphon into bottles, seal and store for three weeks. (Makes about 9 litres/16 pints).

Brown ale

malt syrup	560g/1¼lb	Fuggles hops	14g/½oz
crystal malt grains	110g/4oz	table salt	1g/¼tsp
brown sugar	100g/3½oz	beer yeast	

Dissolve the malt in 2 litres/3½ pints warm water, add the crystal malt and three quarters of the hops. Bring to the boil and continue for 30 minutes. Add the remaining hops and boil for a further five minutes. Leave to cool for 15 minutes.

Strain into a fermentation bin, stir in the salt and sugar and top up with cold boiled water to 4.5 litres/1 gallon. Cover and leave to cool to 20°C/68°F.

Activate a beer yeast in half a cup of tepid water, mix it into the wort and loosely cover.

Next day skim off the dirty froth and stir well; repeat the following day if necessary.

When fermentation is finished, bottle, prime, seal and store as already described. (Makes about 4.5 litres/8 pints.)

Grain mashed beers

Formulating the mash

Having mastered the brewing of beers from malt syrup and hops, it is but a short and simple step to producing wort by mashing and sparging a balanced selection of grains.

First of all prepare a formula of grains and adjuncts, bearing in mind the following factors:

- Crushed pale malt must always be used to provide most of the alcohol in the finished beer. 500 g of pale malt in 5 litres/1 lb in one gallon, when properly mashed and sparged, could give a specific gravity of as much as 1.027. In practice, however, it is not often possible in the home, and 1.024 is more likely, or even a little less.
- To obtain the best extraction rate, mash the pale malt at the rate of 1.5–2.5 kg per 5 litres/3–4 lb per gallon of liquor.
- Sparging to be fully effective should be at the rate of 2.25 litres/half a gallon of liquor per 454 g/1 lb of malt.
- In theory, 3.6 kg/8 lb pale malt could produce a specific gravity of 1.045 in 22.5 litres/5 gallons of liquor, but be pleased to get 1.038.
- For most beers, 15 g/½ oz of the new hop varieties is sufficient to flavour and preserve 4.5 litres/1 gallon of wort. But for beers of high original gravity the hop rate should be slightly increased to balance the malt.
- Any additional sugar used should never provide more than one fifth of the original gravity.

- Crystal malt, although it contributes maltose to a wort, is primarily used to provide colour and flavour; it should, therefore, never exceed one tenth of the pale malt.
- Chocolate and black malts contribute only dark colour and strong flavour to a beer. They should be used only in small quantities and reserved exclusively for brown ales and stouts.
- Roasted barley should be reserved for dry stouts.
- Adjuncts in the form of flakes should not exceed one sixth of the quantity of the pale malt used.
- Flaked maize imparts a dry flavour to a beer.
- Flaked rice imparts a thin dry flavour and should be reserved for pale ales and lagers.
- Flaked barley contributes to head retention.
- Sugar is wholly fermentable into alcohol and carbon dioxide. 500 g dissolved in 5 litres of water/1 lb in 1 gallon, produces a specific gravity of 1.040.
- Grain mashed beers contain unfermentable sugars called dextrins, that provide body and a hint of sweetness. At the end of fermentation, grain mashed beers may have a final gravity as high as 1.008.

Mashing the grains

Having decided on the style and quantity of beer to be made, and selected the proportion of pale malt and other malts and adjuncts, crush or coarsely grind the malts, unless you have bought it already crushed. Place it in your mashing bin and stir in the appropriate quantity of hot liquor. Hard water is best for bitter beers and soft water for brown ales, stouts and lagers. Soft water can be adjusted with hardening salts; hard water with table salt. If chlorine is ever found in your tap water, then you should first boil all the water you use for several minutes, preferably in an open pan, so that the chlorine can be dissipated into the atmosphere. Failure to do this is likely to cause a taste of TCP in the beer, as the chlorine combines with 'phenolics' in the hops.

The striking temperature of the liquor should be higher than the mashing temperature to allow for loss of heat in the pouring and stirring, and the warming up of the grains and the bin itself. Around 75°C/167°F is usually about right for a mashing temperature of 66°C/152°F. The mash should be stirred, then covered and insulated so that the temperature remains as constant as possible. In the home this is extremely difficult, and minor variations cannot be avoided. The first half hour is the most important. After this check the temperature and if it has fallen below 65°C/150°F add 300 ml/half a pint or so of boiling water to restore the original 66°C/152°F. The enzymes that convert the starch to maltose and dextrin are very heat sensitive in the range 64°C/147°F to 67°F/154°F. At the higher end they produce rather more dextrin which contributes to the body of the beer and adds a hint of sweetness. At the lower end slightly more maltose is produced.

After two hours, a check should be made on the progress of the conversion. Remove a level tablespoonful of the mash, place it in a saucer and add a few drops of iodine from the first aid box. If the liquor turns blue or darkens, then some starch still remains and mashing should be continued for another half hour. When no colour change is observed the mash is ready for sparging.

Sparging

Of all the commercial aspects of brewing beer, this is the most difficult to emulate in the home without special equipment. The theory is to drain the liquor from the bottom of the mash whilst slowly spraying the top with a fine shower of hot water. The maltose and dextrin have to be washed out of the grains, not just rinsed off the surface. It is helpful to make some hydrometer checks on the specific gravity of the liquor from time to time. At first the density of the sparging will be quite high, but will gradually fall as the sugars are washed out.

A calico sparging bag and a strong wire stand is quite effective. The bag is first sterilized and then the mash is poured into it. The liquor is collected in a bin beneath. The sparging spray could be a rose attached to a kettle or a small watering can kept for the purpose. The sparging liquor should be hard or soft as required.

Some mashing bins are fitted with a fine grating on which the mash lies and beneath this is a shallow collecting area fitted with an outlet tap. At the end of mashing, the tap can be opened and the liquor run into a boiling pan or copper. The same spray as just described could be used.

Boiling

When all the liquor has been collected, the hops of your choice should be added and thoroughly wetted. Being slightly oily they repel the liquor and have to be squeezed to make them absorb it. All of the hops need not be added at once. Some may be saved to add towards the end of the boil, or even a few during fermentation: the process known as dry hopping. For this purpose hop pellets are very useful since they crumble easily and are quickly absorbed.

A vigorous rolling boil should be maintained so that the hops are constantly moved up and down and round about. This is needed to obtain a good extraction of the hop oils and resins which contribute so much to the flavour and keeping characteristics of the beer. The boil should last for an hour or longer. Towards the end, some fresh hops may be added for the last ten to fifteen minutes to enhance the tang rather than the bitterness of the hops. The quantity of wort may be reduced by the long boil, and some brewers make more wort than they require so that it can be condensed during the boiling.

When the heat is switched off, the wort should be left covered for about half an hour while the proteins coagulate and settle out.

Fermentation

The hops should now be strained out through a calico or fine-meshed nylon straining bag. Any additional cold water or sugar should be mixed in and the wort left covered in a fermentation vessel to cool to 20°C/68°F. The specific gravity should be checked and, if necessary, adjusted.

Some sugar will be required for priming (see also glossary page 133) the finished beer, and a method favoured by some brewers is to draw off 5 per cent (one twentieth) of the unfermented wort and save it for this purpose. It should be stored in a sterilized bottle and kept in the refrigerator until required, about one week later.

An activated yeast should now be well stirred in, not only to distribute the yeast throughout the wort, but also to admit some oxygen into the brew to make up for that lost during the boiling. A loose cover should be placed over the bin which may be left without further attention for 24 hours. By this time, however, the wort will be covered with foam several inches high. It will have many greeny/black and brown specks in it and a brown ring of yeast will be around the inside of the bin. All this must be removed since it contains impurities not wanted in the finished beer. The inclusion of some Irish moss with the hops during the boiling helps to minimize the discoloration of the froth due to hop particles and grain debris.

After the skimming, the wort should be well roused up from the bottom to the top, then covered and left for a further 24 hours. Another head of foam will have formed but this will be closer grained and looking rather like a cauliflower. Again it should be skimmed off and the yeast ring wiped away with a clean tissue. This avoids a bitter yeasty taste in the finished beer. If dry hopping is planned, now is the time to add the fresh hops – no more than a handful – or a few hop pellets. The wort should then be re-covered and left for fermentation to finish – about another five days.

Conditioning

When fermentation is finished, finings may be stirred in but are not essential if the beer can be moved to a cold place for a few days while the insoluble particles settle. It helps to clear the beer if it is siphoned from its pasty deposit into glass demijohns, sealed, and left for a few days in a cold place. It can then be siphoned into bottles or casks, and primed with the unfermented wort or with sugar at the rate of 20 g/¾ oz per 4.5 litres/gallon (half a level teaspoonful per pint). A gap of about 4 cm/1½ in should be left in each bottle in which the gas from the secondary fermentation can collect. The bottles should be sealed with sterilized screw stoppers or crown caps, labelled, and put into a cool store to mature.

Some brewers leave their beers in a warm place while the fermentation takes place, but this is not essential since this beer should be kept for at least one month to mature. Indeed, the author strongly recommends that the beer be kept for three months. Whilst the beer can be consumed earlier and with pleasure, it goes on improving and will keep for a year.

Serving

Before opening them, leave the bottles in the refrigerator for half an hour unless they have been stored in a cold place. The beer should taste cold, but not icy. The bottles should be handled with care and the stopper or cap so removed as not to disturb the sediment. Pour the beer down the side of the glass slowly so that it does not froth. Stop when the sediment reaches the neck of the bottle. Earthenware, pewter or stainless steel tankards may be used and it is said that these keep the beer cooler, but the visual pleasure of seeing the clear beer with its lively bead and creamy head is lost.

Clubs and competitions

There is a common bond between members of most professions, trades and crafts, but in none is this more strongly expressed than in wine-making and brewing. The end products are in themselves conducive to gregariousness, they are best enjoyed when shared with another. Throughout the world this fellowship of winemakers and brewers is quite outstanding, as the author can personally testify.

Clubs

In Great Britain there are more than 1,000 clubs for home wine-makers and brewers. Membership costs only a few pounds per head to pay for the hire of a meeting place once a month. The meetings provide opportunities for members to listen to talks on all the different aspects of making wine, mead, beer, cider and liqueurs at home.

You can ask questions, and there are ample opportunities for tasting each other's brews and evaluating the quality of your own.

Clubs exist in almost every town or large village, as well as in large companies and organizations. Information about the meeting place is usually kept in town halls or public libraries, or the local newspaper office. Sometimes an introduction to a member can be arranged so that you are accompanied to your first meeting.

Some clubs also have a supplies officer who buys certain items in bulk and at a discount which is passed on to the members. There is always some member of the club who has read about, or heard of, some new piece of equipment or method, or where certain ingredients are inexpensively available.

Clubs also organize dinners, dances, barbecues, outings and other social activities for their members. In the late 1970s, visits to vineyards abroad became popular and these include tastings and tours so that members can improve their knowledge about wine.

Many local Education Authorities organize evening classes in wine-making and in wine appreciation. By knowing the standard of quality of different commercial wines of the world, it is easier to assess the quality of wines made in the home. It is clear that some home wine-makers can reach a very high standard indeed and most can equal the European table wines, sometimes referred to unkindly as 'plonk'. Since the homemade equivalent of this wine may have cost no more than one tenth the price, those who make their own wine have a great advantage over those who do not.

Competitions

These can cover a wide range of wine and beer styles, not only at club level but also at county and national level. The wines and beers are objectively evaluated by member of the National Guild of Wine and Beer Judges, who have been specially trained and have proved themselves to be competent wine-makers or brewers by winning trophies at major competitions.

To be admitted to membership of the Guild, candidates must also prove by examination a proper understanding of the theory of wine-making or brewing, and a detailed knowledge of the Guild's handbook. Finally they have to satisfy the examiners at a practical test of tasting a number of wines or beers previously assessed by three Assistant Examiners, that they are able to evaluate them accurately. After judging wines and beers at a competition, members of the Guild are available to give helpful advice to exhibitors.

To exhibit wine or beer in a competition, whether at club, federation, or national level, first obtain a copy of the schedule giving details of the different classes. They usually include dry red and white table wines, sweet table wine, dessert wines, rosé, sparkling and aperitif wines. Sometimes there are special classes for novices, or classes for wines by ingredient, e.g. elderberry, grape concentrate, flowers, etc. Beers usually include bitters, stouts, lagers and barley wines. In the major shows there may be as many as forty different classes, while in the minor shows there may be as few as three.

The schedule will also indicate the style of bottle and stopper to be used, where the label is to be placed, when the entries have to be submitted, and when the exhibits have to be delivered. Read all these details carefully, for at every competition there is always at least one person who enters wine in the wrong class or the wrong bottle, or with the wrong stopper or the label stuck in the wrong place. Remember that this is a competition that affects the eye as well as the nose and the palate. Do avoid silly mistakes through carelessness.

Having read the schedule, look over your wines and beers and consider for which classes you have suitable entries. Pick out the chosen bottles and set them aside. Send off your entry to the secretary and as soon as your labels arrive, prepare your bottles. The label will bear the number allocated to the class and the exhibit number allocated to you. The first number enables the competition steward to put all the wines or beers of the same class in the same place. The exhibitor's number is known only to you and the competition secretary.

Check that the labels are correct and check again that the wines and beers that you wish to enter not only correspond to the class labels received but also to the classes listed in the schedule that you decided to enter.

Wines must be shown in colourless glass, punted bottles with rounded shoulders. Cork stoppers must be used and the bottle should be filled to within 2 cm/¾ in of the bottom of the stopper. All bottles must be moulded and the two halves are stuck together forming a seam at both sides. The identification label must be stuck equidistant between the seams and not nearer to one than the other, nor across one of them since this would diminish the visual aspect. It should be stuck on at the right height from the bottom of the bottle prescribed in the schedule.

Before filling your cleaned and sterilized bottle, inspect the wine or beer once again, and make sure that it is suitable for entry. It should be star bright and free from sediment or floating particles. It should smell and taste clean and be dry or sweet, according to the class. Seal the bottles, wipe them clean, wrap them in tissue paper and deliver them, when required, to the steward.

To the judge your bottle is only identified by a number. Total confidentiality is maintained and since the Guild began, in 1964, the integrity of a judge has never been questioned. You may be quite sure that prizes will be awarded solely on the merits of the exhibits.

Whether you win an award or not, do take the opportunity to have a word with the judges of the classes you entered. Beside your exhibit number on his or her record sheet, he or she will have written the number of points given your exhibit for presentation, clarity, colour, bouquet and taste, as well as some remarks. By giving your exhibit number, the judges can consult their records and discuss the exhibit with you. There is much to learn, and no one knows it all.

In most classes, there are usually a few outstanding wines, closely followed by a half or two-thirds of the rest that can be classified as a good average. The remainder are less attractive and there may even be a few that are diseased and too foul smelling to taste. One wonders why such wines or beers are entered for they should have been thrown away. Lack of hygiene, poor ingredients and poor methods will never make good wine or beer.

If you are in the top two-thirds you have the satisfaction of knowing that a competent judge has thought well of your wine and this enhances the pleasure of drinking it with your friends, and talking about the ingredients and methods used. Not only is talking with your friends about good wine, mead, beer and cider you have made yourself one of the great pleasures of the world, but joining a wine- and beer-makers' club is also one of the best ways of meeting friends who share your interest.

Index